Afterlife
The Whol

Life After Death Books I & II

From Ernie —
December 2021

**Other books by
Stephen Hawley Martin**

*The Secret of Life
Accept It, Embrace It, Discover Pure Joy*

*The Truth about Life
And How to Make Yours the Best of All*

*The True Holy Grail
The Secret You Can Use to Create the Life You Want*

*Edgar Cayce,
The Meaning of Life and What to Do About It*

*Bewitched?
A Startling New Theory of the Cause
of the Salem Witch Hysteria from the
Descendant of a Woman Hanged*

*Actual Magic
The Secret to Manifesting Your Desires*

*ESP
How I Developed My Sixth Sense
And So Can You*

*The Luciferian Candidate
A Paranormal Adventure*

*The Search for Nina Fletcher
You Won't Put This Book Down Until She Is Found*

*The Secret of Life
An Adventure Out of Body, Into Mind*

*Death in Advertising
A Whodunit*

Afterlife,
The Whole Truth
Life After Death Books I & II

Stephen Hawley Martin

WWW.OAKLEAPRESS.COM

Afterlife, The Whole Truth: Life After Death Books I & II © 2021 by The Oaklea Press. All rights reserved. No part of this book may be used or reproduced in any manner whatsoever without written permission except in the case of brief quotations embodied in critical articles and reviews. For information visit: www.OakleaPress.com.

To see a listing of the author's most popular books, follow this link:

https://www.shmartin.com/home

Note: This two-book volume contains *Life After Death, Powerful Evidence You Will Never Die* and its sequel, *Life After Death Book II, Heaven, Hell, & You.*

LIFE AFTER DEATH BOOK I: POWERFUL EVIDENCE

Foreword 9

Chapter One
Consciousness and the Brain 13

Chapter Two
True Stories of Consciousness Outside the Body 29

Chapter Three
Awareness Is Non Local 43

Chapter Four
Proof of Accurate Information about the Dead 62

Chapter Five
Evidence from the Past Consciousness Continues 83

Chapter Six
More than Fifty Years of Irrefutable Research 93

Chapter Seven
Life Between Lives 115

Chapter Eight
The Cosmology of Soul Evolution 133

Chapter Nine
The Science of Reincarnation 142

Chapter Ten
How Non-Physical Reality May Form the Physical 156

Chapter Eleven
Why Accepting the Truth Can Be Difficult 172

Chapter Twelve
High Time for a Paradigm Shift 182

Chapter Thirteen
A New Worldview 202

LIFE AFTER DEATH BOOK II: HEAVEN, HELL, & YOU

Preface 218

Chapter One
How We Got Here 218

Chapter Two
Heaven Explored 232

Chapter Three
What Heaven Is Like 240

Chapter Four
The Stages of Spiritual Growth 251

Chapter Five
Making a Conscious Decision to Grow 259

Chapter Six
Be Truthful to Yourself and Others 267

Chapter Seven
Always Have and Pursue a Challenge 271

Chapter Eight
Follow Your Bliss 276

Chapter Nine
A Few More Thoughts & Truths 285

Chapter Ten
Where Will You Go from Here? 289

Books by the Author You Might Like 308

Life After Death Book I
Powerful Evidence
You Will Never Die

"Anyone who has had an experience of mystery knows that there is a dimension of the universe that is not that which is available to his senses."

— Joseph Campbell (1904-1987)

Foreword

I have two primary objectives for this book.

First is to demonstrate that you are eternal. Your body will someday die, but your consciousness will live on. You see, you are spirit, what I will call "life force," that has come into the physical dimension for a reason. I hope this book will encourage you to find the particular reason you came here at the time and place you did.

Second, I would like this book to help establish a new worldview. The western world is long overdue for such a shift. The current worldview, which had its origins with the English philosopher Thomas Hobbes in the seventeenth century, is that the universe, the solar system and our bodies, can be compared to machines. Everything is separate, and even our bodies and our minds are assemblies of separate parts. It seems incredibly odd to me that we would have this materialistic worldview at a time when physicists assure us that no such thing as solid or separate stuff exists. Everything we can see, touch, or feel is energy—vibrations. You are energy. I am energy. All is energy.

With this in mind, I respectfully request that you make an effort to suspend disbelief as you read ahead. Support for my thesis will unfold and build as the chapters roll by.

What, then, is my thesis? It is that all is one, that there is one mind from which everything in the universe, including you and me, emanates. It is that through a natural process, this one mind has become subdivided so that we each have our own unique consciousness and perspective. But, nonetheless, we remain connected to and an integral aspect of the one mind.

In addition to stating my objectives, I would also like to use this space to offer an apology. The terminology I have elected to use for what I refer to alternatively as the Universal Mind, the life force, subjective mind, Tao, and ground of being may be offensive to some and confusing to others. All these terms refer to the same thing, or perhaps more accurately, to aspects of the same thing. Perhaps, some day science will come up with a single term we can all readily understand.

Those of a religious bent may believe I should have used the word, God. In some cases I have done so. But for the most part I have avoided this because I know it carries negative connotations for some and for others it conjures up an image that would be misleading. While I agree it is likely we are (metaphorically speaking) created in God's image, there is no man with a long white beard up there sitting on a cloud, picking winners and losers.

How do I know what you also will soon know? I grew up in a secular household. My parents considered anything beyond that which could be measured by a yardstick or viewed under a microscope pure fiction. But I was never quite so sure. My curiosity about such things intensified when I was in my twenties and something happened, what you might call a paranormal experience that raised major doubts in my mind about my family's materialistic worldview—the same worldview most of my college professors held. I became fascinated with metaphysics as a result, and in 2007 took the opportunity to be the talk show host and producer of an Internet radio show called *The Truth about Life*.

For two years I read and interviewed authors engaged in quests for truth. Among them were medical doctors, parapsychologists, metaphysicians, quantum physicists, near death survivors, theologians, psychiatrists, psychologists, and all manner of researchers into the true nature of reality. What I learned led me to what I think is an accurate view of things, and I have to say it's exhilarating to feel I may be on the cutting edge. As best I can tell, this new way of seeing the world is rapidly replacing the materialistic view that has held sway in the scientific community for at least a couple of centuries—ever since Thomas Hobbes' materialistic view of reality took hold and spawned the Age of Enlightenment.

With this book, I'd like to welcome you into a brand new Age of Enlightenment. Read on and join me on the cutting edge of knowledge about the true nature of existence.

Stephen Hawley Martin

"[Scientific Materialists say] give us one free miracle and we'll explain the rest.' And the one free miracle is the appearance of all the matter and energy of the universe, and all the laws that govern it, from nothing in a single instant."

British Biochemist Rupert Sheldrake

Chapter One
Consciousness and the Brain

What if you knew you would exist forever? Would it change your outlook? Would you do anything differently? Would it make you happy? Sad? Uneasy? Would it cause you to want to work on yourself to become someone you would not mind being with forever? I think it's true—you are eternal. Why do I think so? In my book, *Amazing Truth,* I present the findings of quantum physics experiments that any fair-minded person would have to agree is powerful evidence consciousness is the ground of being of reality. Your consciousness, and that ground-of-being consciousness, are one and the same. All of us, and everything else, arose from it. Our consciousness does not result from electrons jumping across synapses in the brain. The brain is merely a receiver that connects our consciousness to our bodies. As a result, we are eternal.

To convince you of this, I'm going to summarize a lecture recorded on video given in India in 2011 by Bruce Greyson, M.D., The Chester Carlson Professor of Psychiatry and Director of the Division of Perceptual Studies at the University of Virginia. His job is to study consciousness and what he has to say about it may open your eyes to the truth.

The bottom line takeaway of Dr. Greyson's lecture is that brains do not actually create consciousness, despite what many scientists still think. He does say, however, that this mistaken belief is understandable since evidence does exist that the brain produces consciousness. Consider what happens when a person drinks too much or gets knocked on the head. Also, it's possible to measure electrical activity in the brain during certain kinds of mental tasks and to identify correlations between different areas of the brain and the different activities. We can stimulate different parts of the brain and record what experiences result, and we can remove parts of the brain and observe the results on behavior. This suggests that the brain is involved with thinking, perception, and memory, but according to Dr. Greyson, it does not necessarily suggest the brain causes those thoughts, perceptions, and memories. What the measurements actually show are correlations, rather than causation. The truth is that thoughts, perceptions, and memories, actually occur somewhere else and then are received and processed by the brain in a way similar to how a television, cell phone, or radio receiver works.

Western science, Dr. Greyson pointed out, is largely reductionist. It breaks everything down to its component parts, which are much easier to study than the whole, but the component parts do not always act like the whole. The brain is composed of millions of nerve cells or neurons, but a single neuron cannot formulate a thought, cannot feel angry or cold. It appears that brains can think and feel, but brain cells cannot. No one knows how many neurons are needed in order for them to collectively formulate a thought, nor do we know how a collection of neurons can think when a single neuron cannot.

Scientists get around this by saying consciousness is an emergent property of brains, a property that emerges when a large enough mass of brain cells gets together. According to Dr. Greyson, however, saying something is an emergent property is a way of saying it is a mystery that cannot be explained. It is a fact that there is no known mechanism in the brain or anywhere else that can produce non-physical things like thoughts, memories, or perceptions. The materialistic understanding of the world fails to deal with how electrical impulses, or a chemical trigger in the brain, can produce a thought or a feeling, or for that matter, anything the mind does. Despite this, according to Dr. Greyson, most scientists continue to maintain what he labeled, "The nineteenth century, materialist view that the brain in some miraculous way we do not understand produces consciousness." These scientists, he said, "Discount or ignore that consciousness in extreme circumstances can function very well without a brain."

Dr. Greyson noted that the idea the mind and the brain are separate is what most people believed until a couple of hundred years ago, but in the nineteenth century western world, beginning with the Darwinians, science began exploring the idea that the physical brain might be the source of thoughts and consciousness. Ironically, as one group of scientists attempted to explain consciousness in terms of Newtonian physics, scientists in a different discipline, physics, were forced to move away from Newtonian physics and develop quantum mechanics in order to explain phenomena in which consciousness—what a researcher knows or doesn't know—completely changes the results of certain experiments. It is as though the right hand did not know what the left hand was up to. Incredibly, this remains how things are today.

Dr. Greyson listed a number of examples in his lecture of evidence researchers with the Division of Perceptual Studies—established in 1967 at the University of Virginia—have collected that demonstrate that consciousness can exist without a brain being involved. It is a testament to the stubbornness of materialist scientists that even though Dr. Greyson and his colleagues have been collecting this data for fifty years, and many papers and books have been written and published revealing a great deal of it, most western scientists are unaware of this evidence. As a result, you will soon have a leg up on many western scientists.

The evidence falls into four categories:

1. Recovery of lost consciousness in the moments or days prior to death among people who have been unconscious for prolonged periods of time.
2. Complex consciousness ability in some people who have minimal brain tissue.
3. Complex consciousness in near-death experiences when the brain is not functioning or is functioning at a greatly diminished level.
4. Memories, particularly among young children, accurately recalling details of a past life.

Deathbed recovery of lost consciousness

The unexpected return of mental clarity shortly before death by patients suffering from neurological or psychiatric disorders has been reported in western medical literature for more than 250 years. There are published cases in the medical literature of patients suffering from brain abscesses, tumors, stokes, meningitis, Alzheimer's disease, schizophrenia, and mood disorders, all of whom long before had lost the ability to think or communicate. In many of these cases, evidence from brain scans or autopsies showed their brains had deteriorated to an irreversible degree, and yet in all of them, mental clarity returned in the last minutes, hours, and sometimes days before the patients' deaths. The Division of Perceptual Studies has identified 83 cases in western medical literature and has collected additional unpublished contemporary accounts wherein patients recovered complete consciousness just before death. It appears as though the damaged brain released its grip on a patient's mind and clarity returned as a result.

In 1844, a German psychiatrist named Julius reported that this occurred in 13 percent of patients who had died in his institution. In a recent investigation of end of life experiences in the United Kingdom, 70 percent of caregivers in nursing homes reported that they had observed patients suffering from dementia and confusion becoming completely lucid in their last hours before death. In a case Dr. Greyson himself investigated, a 42-year-old man developed a malignant brain tumor that rapidly grew in size. He quickly became bedridden, blind in one eye, unable to communicate, incoherent and bizarre in this behavior. He appeared unable to make any sense of his surroundings, and when members of his family touched him, he would slap as through being annoyed by an insect. He eventually stopped sleeping and would talk deliriously throughout the night making no sense. After several weeks of this, he suddenly appeared calm and began speaking coherently. He then slept peacefully. The following morning, he remained completely clear and talked with his wife, discussing his imminent death for the first time. He then stopped speaking and died.

There is no known physiological mechanism to explain this phenomenon. It is rare, but the fact that it happens has no explanation in terms of how the brain functions. It suggests the link between consciousness and the brain is more complex that most scientists think. It is as though the damaged brain prevents the person from communicating, but when the brain finally begins to die, consciousness is released from the degenerating brain.

Complex consciousness among people who have minimal brain tissue

Another phenomenon is the presence of normal or even high intelligence in people who have very little brain tissue. There are rare but surprising cases of people who seem to function normally, with normal intelligence, and normal social function, despite having virtually no brain at all. In one case, published in 2007, a high school honor student who had been accepted for enrollment by Smith College underwent surgery after she was injured and knocked unconscious in an automobile accident. An x-ray of her head just before surgery revealed that she had no cerebral cortex at all. She had just a brainstem inside her skull. When the surgeon opened her skull to operate that is exactly what he found—a brainstem and that's all.

Neurologists tell us the brainstem relays motor and sensory signals to the cerebellum and the spinal cord and integrates heart function, breathing, wakefulness, and animal functions. They also tell us the brainstem does not have the connections to perform higher cognitive functions such as thinking, perceiving, making decisions, and so forth. According to scientific knowledge as it now stands, this college-bound honor student should not have been able to formulate a thought of any kind, let alone function at a high intellectual level.

Hers is not an isolated situation. Dr. Greyson pointed to dozens of cases of patients with hydrocephalus, wherein as much as 95 percent of a brain is incapacitated due to an excess of cerebrospinal fluid, and yet many with that level of affliction have normal and even above average intelligence.

Near Death Experiences

The near death experiences [NDEs] Dr. Greyson covered in the lecture were accounts given by people who had been clinically dead for a short time and then resuscitated or revived spontaneously. He said they typically have memories of vivid sensory imagery, and an extremely clear memory of what they experienced. They often describe what they experienced as seeming "more real" than their everyday life. All of this occurs under conditions of drastically altered brain function under which the materialist model would say is absolutely impossible. Such memories are reported by between ten and twenty percent of those who are revived from clinical death. Dr. Greyson has personally investigated almost one thousand cases.

The average age at the time of the near death in these cases was 31 years, but there was a very wide range. A young girl reported an experience she'd had at eight months old while undergoing kidney surgery. The oldest to experience near death Dr. Greyson has studied was 81 at the time of his heart attack. About one third of the NDEs occurred during surgical operations, a quarter during serious illness, and another quarter as a result of life-threatening accidents. The common features of NDEs can be categorized as changes in thinking, changes in emotional state, as well as paranormal and otherworldly features.

Changes in thinking include a sense of time being altered. Often people report that time stopped or ceased to exist. The change in thinking phenomenon also included a sudden revelation or change in understanding in which everything in the universe suddenly became crystal clear. There was a sense of the person's thoughts going much faster and being much clearer than usual. Finally, there was a life review—a panoramic memory in which the person's life seemed to flash before him or her.

Typical emotions reported included an overwhelming sense of peace and wellbeing, a sense of cosmic unity and of being one with everything, a feeling of complete joy, and a sense of being loved unconditionally.

The paranormal features included a sense of leaving the physical body, sometimes called an out of body experience [OBE], a sense of physical senses such as seeing and hearing becoming more vivid than ever before. Sometimes people report seeing colors and hearing sounds that do no exist in this life, and a sense of extrasensory perception, i.e., of knowing things beyond the normal ability of the senses, such as things that are happening at a remote location. Finally, some report having visions of the future and that they entered another, unearthly world or realm of existence.

Many report they came to a border they could not cross, a point of no return that if they had crossed they would not be able to return to life. Many also say they encountered a mystical or divine being, and some report seeing spirits and loved ones who died previously and seem to be welcoming them into another realm, or in some cases sending them back to life.

Life After Death

As a psychiatrist, the profound after effects of NDEs are of particular interest to Dr. Greyson. Near death survivors reliably report a consistent pattern of changes in attitudes, beliefs, and values, which do not seem to fade over time. They report overwhelmingly they are more spiritual because of their experience, that they have more compassion, a greater desire to help others, a greater appreciation for life as well as a stronger sense of meaning and purpose in life. An overwhelming majority reports they have a stronger belief that we survive death of the body and no longer have any fear of death. About half report they have lost interest in material possessions, and many report they no longer have an interest in obtaining personal prestige, status, or in competition.

Dr. Greyson said that three features of NDEs suggest consciousness is not produced by the brain: 1) Enhanced mental function while the brain is incapacitated; 2) Accurate perceptions from outside the body, such as the ability to accurately tell doctors and nurses what they saw and heard going on in the operating room; and 3) encounters with deceased persons who convey accurate information no one else could have known, including in some instances encounters with deceased persons the NDE survivor could not have known were dead at the time.

In one case, a nine-year-old boy with meningitis had an NDE in which he saw several deceased relatives, including his sister who told him he had to return to his body. As soon as he returned from death, he told his parents—who had been at his bedside for 36 hours during his ordeal. His father became very upset because his daughter was at college in a different state and was perfectly healthy as far as the father knew. The boy insisted that his sister had sent him back and had told him she had to remain.

The father left the hospital, promising his wife he would call their daughter as soon as he got home. When he tried to call her, he learned that the college officials had been trying to contact him and his wife all night to tell them the tragic news. Their daughter had been killed in an automobile accident around midnight.

By the way, a video of Dr. Greyson's lecture just summarized can be viewed by searching YouTube using the following phrase: "Dr Bruce Greyson Consciousness Independent of the Brain."

Children Who Recall a Past Life

Dr. Greyson also recounted information about the Division of Perceptual Studies' research into children's memories of past lives. Researchers at the University of Virginia have been conducting these investigations for more than fifty years and as a result have in excess of 2500 cases in their files. I was quite familiar with this even before I saw Dr. Greyson's lecture because of research I had done for my book, *REINCARNATION: Good News for Open Minded Christians and Other Truth Seekers.* I have in fact twice interviewed one of the Perceptual Division's key researchers who has written two books on the Division's reincarnation research findings, Jim B. Tucker, M.D., a child psychiatrist.

Anyone with an open mind who looks into what has been found will find it difficult to refute that reincarnation can and does happen. To give you a taste, I will relate a fascinating case history I also reported on in the book just mentioned. This true story began on the First of May 2000.

Imagine you and your wife [or husband] are sound asleep. Your two-year-old son James is in his crib, asleep in the next room. Suddenly you are jarred awake.

You hear your son scream, "Plane on fire! Airplane crash!"

You rush into his room, and there he is on the bed, writhing the grip of horror, kicking and clawing at the covers as if he is trying to kick his way out of a coffin.

Over and over again, your child screams, "Plane on fire! Little man can't get out!"

What happened that night was not a single occurrence. Traumatic nightly scenes like it became the norm. The nightmares became even more terrifying, and James started screaming the name of the "little man" who couldn't get out of the plane. It was "James," his own name. Other words he spoke out loud included: "Jack Larsen," "Natoma" and "Corsair."

James' father, Bruce Leininger, could not think of what to do. Eventually, in attempt to find an answer to his son's troubled nights, he embarked on a research project, armed only with the names and words his son had been shouting while in a disturbed sleep.

A devote Christian, the answer Bruce found was not the one he wanted. He came to believe his son James was the reincarnation of a World War Two fighter pilot whose plane had been hit and downed by antiaircraft fire—a pilot named James Huston who had died in 1945 after his plane suffered a direct hit and crashed.

James' mother, however, was the first to suspect the truth. At the time, James was having five nightmares a week, and his mother, Andrea, was worried. At a toy shop, Andrea and James were looking at model planes.

"Look," Andrea said. "There's a bomb on the bottom of that one."

"That's not a bomb, Mommy," James said. "That's a drop tank."

The child was two years old. How could he possibly have known about the gas tank used by aircraft in World War Two to extend their range?

As the nightmares continued, Andrea asked, "Who is the 'little man'?"

"Me," he answered.

Bruce asked, "What happened to your plane?"

"It crashed on fire."

"Why did your plane crash?"

"It got shot," James said.

"Who shot your plane?"

"The Japanese!" he said.

James said he knew it was the Japanese because of "the big red sun." He was, of course, describing the Japanese symbol of the rising sun painted on their warplanes.

Andrea began to suggest reincarnation. Wouldn't that explain it? But Bruce reacted angrily. He thought there must be a rational explanation, and reincarnation was definitely not in his mind a rational explanation.

Bruce questioned his son further. "Do you remember what kind of plane the little man flew?"

"A Corsair," two-year-old James replied without hesitation. It was a word he had shouted in his dreams.

Bruce knew a Corsair was a World War Two fighter plane.

"Where did your airplane take off?" Bruce asked.

"A boat."

"What was the name of the boat?"

James replied with certainty, "The Natoma."

Bruce did some research. He was amazed to find the Natoma Bay was a World War Two aircraft carrier. Bruce rushed to his office, where he had a dictionary of American naval fighting ships. Natoma Bay had supported the U.S. Marines' invasion of Iwo Jima in 1945.

Andrea, meanwhile, had become convinced James was reincarnated. She contacted Carol Bowman, the author of a book on reincarnation and children who remember past lives. Bowman confirmed Andrea's views, saying that the common threads were there with James, including his age when the nightmares began and his remembered death.

Bruce kept investigating. He decided to see if he could find someone named Jack Larsen, a name James had shouted repeatedly during his nightmares. Bruce was successful in finding someone who fit the time period and place. It turned out Larsen's friend James Huston had died when his plane was shot in the engine and caught fire, just as had been described by two-year-old James Leininger.

Bruce also found Huston's name on the list of 18 men killed in action on the Natoma. The discovery finally made him realize his son might actually be the reincarnation of James Huston. But he kept investigating, anyway, and everything he found served to confirm that conclusion.

One day, little James unnerved his father when he said, "I knew you would be a good daddy, that's why I picked you."

"Where did you find us?" asked an incredulous Bruce.

"In Hawaii, at the pink hotel on the beach," James said, and went on to describe his parents' fifth wedding anniversary, which had taken place five weeks before Andrea had gotten pregnant. James said that was when he "chose" the couple to bring him back into the world.

Something new emerged almost every day. On a map, James pointed out the exact location where James Huston's plane went down. Asked why he called his action figures "Billy," "Leon" and "Walter," he replied, "Because that's who met me when I got to heaven."

Eventually, the family received a phone call from a veteran who had seen Huston's plane get hit. The man had kept his knowledge to himself for more than 50 years. He described seeing the aftermath of Huston's crash on the sea below.

"He took a direct hit on the nose. All I could see were pieces falling into the bay. We pulled out of the dive and headed for open sea. I saw the place where the fighter had hit. The rings were still expanding near a huge rock at the harbor entrance."

And so it was as James had said. His plane was hit in the engine and the front exploded in a ball of flames, but that was not the end of James. He returned to this reality fifty-three years later, in 1998, with his memory intact. Perhaps he had some things here on earth he wanted to do, like flying airplanes.

How about you? Whether you come back to this world, stay in the next or move on to another, like it our not you will continue to exist. Now that you know, what is the best thing to do? Become the person you were meant to be and the person you want to be. That person is someone you will probably enjoy being around, which is a good thing, because you are going to be around that person—forever.

Chapter Two
True Stories of Consciousness Outside the Body

Pam Reynolds was only 35 years old when she was told she was going to die.

She'd been suffering dizziness and loss of speech, so her doctor had ordered a CAT scan. Huge aneurysms—two ballooned arteries—were found at the base of her brain near where the stem entered her spine. It would only be a matter of time before one burst. When that happened, Pam's life would come to an end.

Surgery seemed out of the question. One aneurysm was in an almost impossible place to reach without injuring the brain. If the skull were opened, the brain would be in the way—between the aneurysm and the doctor's scalpel.

As good fortune would have it, one long shot possibility did exist. Dr. Robert Spetzler, chief of neurosurgery at the Barrow Neurological Institute in Phoenix, Arizona, offered a radical procedure that would require shutting down Pam's body. Her heart would be stopped. Her body temperature would be lowered to sixty degrees Fahrenheit so there would be little or no deterioration of tissue. The blood would be drained from her brain, and then—only then, because he would in effect be working on a cadaver—Dr. Spetzler could deal with the most difficult to reach aneurysm.

Incredible as it may seem, Pam would literally be dead. If

anyone ever wanted to construct an experiment to find out what happens when we die, this would have been it—provided, of course, Pam actually came back from death to tell the tale.

The procedure was awfully scary, but it was her only chance, so Pam went ahead with it. With no blood running through her brain, the aneurysm would deflate, and the doctor would be able to repair it. Once repaired, the plan was for the surgical team to pump blood back into her through a device that would raise its temperature and along with it, that of her body. Then they would jolt her heart back to life using electric shocks.

Imagine how Pam must have felt when they wheeled her into the operating room on the gurney, wheels squeaking. That was at 7:15 a.m. on August 8, 1991. Anesthesia was administered, both ear channels were occluded with molded ear speakers designed to monitor brain stem function. These clicked constantly. An electroencephalogram (EEG) was set up to monitor cortical brain waves, and an electrical device was affixed to test the functioning of her cerebral hemispheres. These machines would display flat lines once her heart was stopped and her blood drained out.

Pam remembers none of this and remained unconscious until she heard a buzzing sound at 8:40 a.m.—an unpleasant sound, she recalls, reminiscent of a dentist's drill.

Recounting this she said, "I remember the top of my head tingling, and I just sort of popped out of it. Then, I was looking down at my body. I knew it was my body, but for some reason I didn't care.

"My vantage point was that of sitting on the doctor's shoulder. He had an instrument in his hand that looked like an electric toothbrush. That puzzled me. I had assumed they would open the skull with a saw—I'd heard the term 'saw'—but what he was working with looked a lot more like a drill than a saw—sort of like my electric toothbrush—and there also was a case, like the one my father stored his socket wrenches in when I was a child—with little bits in it."

All this turned out to be true. The saw used by the doctor did look like an electric toothbrush, and there was a case with bits in it. The extraordinary thing is, Pam could not have made these observations about tools as she entered the operating room because she would not have been able to see them. All the instruments, including the drill-like saw, were concealed inside sterile packaging, as is standard practice. To maintain a sterile environment, these packages are not opened until the patient is completely asleep.

"I also heard people talking," she continued. "I distinctly remember hearing a female voice say, 'We have a problem. The arteries are too small.'

"Someone said to try the other side.

"This [talking] seemed to come from somewhere down at the other end of the table and I wondered, *What are they doing? This is brain surgery [not surgery on the legs].*

"I later found out they accessed the femoral arteries, which are in the groin area, in order to drain the blood from my body."

Operation records show that the artery first accessed for this purpose could not be used because it was indeed too small, so the artery on the other side was used. Dr. Spetzler verified that no one would be able to hear or see anything, using the usual bodily senses, while in the state Pam Reynolds was in at the time.

But Pam did hear and see what was going on. Her consciousness was outside her body. But it didn't remain in the operating room as surgery progressed.

"I felt a presence, and I turned around to look at it," she said. "That's when I saw a tiny pinpoint of light.

"It [the light] started to pull me. There was a physical sensation like what you might have in your stomach when you drive fast over a hill. So I went toward the light, and as I came closer I began to discern different figures.

"I distinctly heard my grandmother call me. She had a very distinct voice, and I immediately went to her. It felt great. And I saw an uncle who had passed away when he was only 39 years old. He had taught me a lot. He taught me to play my first guitar. I saw many people I knew and many I did not know.

"I asked if God was the light, and the answer was, 'No, God is not the light. The light is what happens when God breathes.' And I remember thinking, I'm standing in the breath of God.

"At some point I was reminded that it was time to go back. Of course, I'd made my decision to go back before the operation, but the more I was there in the light, the more I liked it.

"But my uncle escorted me back down the tunnel.

"When I got to where the body was, and I looked at it, I really did not want to get in it. I was certain about that because it looked like what it was—void of life. And I knew it would hurt.

"But my uncle kept reasoning with me. He said not to worry and go ahead. It would be like diving into a swimming pool.

"'Just jump in,' he said.

"'No,' I said.

"'What about the children?'

"'You know, I think the children will be just fine.'

"'Honey, you've got to go.'

"'No.'

"I saw the body jump.

"Then he pushed me, and I felt [my body] jump.

"It took me a long time, but I guess I'm ready [now] to forgive him for that."

The jump Pam saw, and the one she felt, were caused by the electric shocks to restart her heart.

All this happened under extremely controlled conditions when every known vital sign, every clinical sign of life, and death, was being monitored. Her body had been dead, but her consciousness had lived on.

The doctors have no explanation. They know of no way to explain what Pam experienced given the paradigm science operates within at this time in history. Pam's ability to recall and accurately describe what was going on in the operating room while she was dead with the blood drained from her head and most of her body, indicates her mind had separated from her brain. But today's generally accepted scientific reasoning holds that there can be no memory of anything when the heart is stopped and the brain is not functioning. The only logical explanation is that her consciousness was outside her brain and the memories of her experiences formed there as well.

If this were an isolated case, perhaps it could be dismissed as some sort of anomaly. Certainly, skeptics would try. But there are many, many others. Once such is that reported by Dr. Melvin E. Morse, M.D.

The Case of Kristle Merzlock

In spring, 1982, Kristle Merzlock arrived at the hospital in Pocatello, Idaho, in a coma—having been pulled from the bottom of a swimming pool. Her heart had stopped beating 19 minutes earlier.

Bill Longhurst, the physician who received Kristle in the emergency room, quickly summoned Melvin Morse, then 27, the only doctor at the hospital who'd performed a significant number of resuscitations. Miraculously, he was able to get her heart going and put her on an artificial lung machine.

Morse had topflight academic credentials—a medical degree with honors from George Washington University and a research fellowship funded by the National Cancer Institute. Even so, he was not prepared for what was about to happen. Kristle's pupils were fixed and dilated and she had no gag reflex. A CAT scan revealed massive swelling of her brain, an artificial lung was doing her breathing, and her blood pH was extremely acidic, a clear indication of imminent death. Morse said, "There was little we could do at that point."

But somehow, against all odds, Kristle survived. Three days later she came out of her coma with full brain function. Needless to say, Morse was amazed. But something else amazed him even more and, eventually, forced him to completely rearrange his thinking about consciousness and life after death.

Kristle recognized him.

"That's the one with the beard," she told her mother. "First there was this tall doctor who didn't have a beard, and then he came in."

This was true. Morse had a beard, and the admitting doctor, Longhurst, was clean-shaven and tall.

Kristle then described the emergency room with astonishing accuracy.

Morse said, "She had the right equipment, the right number of people—everything was just as it had been that day." She correctly related the procedures that had been performed on her. Even though her eyes had been closed and she had been profoundly comatose during the entire experience, she still 'saw' what was going on."

Kristle was able to do this, she said, because she was outside her body—that is, her mind and awareness were outside floating above it, observing what was going on. As you might expect, Morse had a hard time believing what she told him about her out-of-body experience (OBE), and his skepticism showed through. Kristle patted him shyly on the hand and said, "Don't worry, Dr. Morse, heaven is fun!"

Morse wrote up her case for the American Medical Association's Pediatric Journal as a "fascinoma," meaning a strange yet interesting case. Then he returned to cancer research. One night, he saw Elizabeth Kübler-Ross on television describing to a grieving mother what her child went through when she died. Kübler-Ross said that the girl floated out of her body, suffered no pain, and entered into heaven. Morse thought this was unprofessional of a psychiatrist, and vowed to prove her wrong.

NDE Research by Morse and Sharp

He teamed up with Kimberly Clark Sharp, a clinical social worker in Seattle to begin researching near-death experiences (NDEs) in children. Their work later became known as The Seattle Study. At Seattle Children's Hospital, they designed and implemented the first prospective study of NDEs with age and sex matched controls. They studied 26 children who nearly died and compared them to 131 children who were also quite ill, in the intensive care unit, mechanically ventilated, treated with drugs such as morphine, Valium and anesthetic agents. Often they had suffered a lack of oxygen to the brain, but none had ever reached the near-death state of actually being clinically dead.

Before 1976, not much had been published on NDEs, but that year a medical student named Raymond Moody published what became a best-selling book called Life After Life. Moody interviewed patients who had been resuscitated after being clinically dead and described what he found to be common occurrences in such instances: a sensation of serenity, separation from the body, entrance into a dark tunnel, a vision of light, and the appearance of deceased family members who offer help.

Morse said working with kids had its advantages. "The adult near-death experience is cluttered by cultural references and contaminated by the need for validation," he explained. "But with kids, it's pure. Kids don't repress the memory, or fear the ridicule that might come from talking about it."

He found that of the 26 children who nearly died 23 had NDEs whereas none of the other children had them. If NDEs are caused by a lack of oxygen to the brain, drugs, hallucinations secondary to coma, or stress and the fear of dying, then the control would have been expected to have also experienced NDEs, but they did not, indicating that NDEs happen only to the dying.

Morse was determined, he said, to "produce a study that would hold up under the most stringent peer review." He pored over the medical records of each patient, documenting the drugs they took, the anesthesia used on them and the level of oxygen in their blood. His team of medical students combed the literature in search of reports of drug use, psychological states or oxygen deprivation that might have produced hallucinations similar to near-death experiences.

When he published his results in the *American Journal of Diseases of Children,* Morse felt he was on solid ground in asserting near-death experiences are not the result of drugs or sleep deprivation, nor are they merely dreams or hallucinations. He was extremely careful to stay on firm scientific ground, labeling them "natural psychological processes associated with dying." While he could not explain what caused NDEs, he could prove that something consistent was going on, something that could not be explained in medical terms.

If you think Morse's colleagues and the medical community toasted him, and gave him a pat on the back, you are wrong. Morse was ridiculed and scorned by other doctors. Soon, prominent physicians questioned whether he could even deliver good patient care.

What I call "pseudo skeptics" have advanced a number of theories to explain the visions of dying patients. I call them pseudo skeptics because they will come up with almost ridiculous ways to attempt to shoot down what is clearly obvious based on solid data. Some attributed the NDEs to "anesthetic agents" administered in the hospital, even though Morse found that many of the subjects studied were dying far from a hospital setting. Others considered the visions to be hallucinations produced by narcotics, endorphins or profound oxygen deprivation—none of which, Morse insists, have been shown to correlate with the near death experiences he documented. He believes the medical community rejected his conclusions for a variety of reasons—one being his willingness to talk about death as a positive experience.

He said, "There's a feeling that people come to doctors to keep living, that if death is treated as a result that isn't necessarily negative, then we may not do all we can to avoid it."*

This does not ring true to me. I believe a small percentage of scientists with a vested interest in maintaining the status quo have intimidated the majority into holding on the old paradigm that says consciousness cannot exist outside the brain. We will soon look at studies that clearly show that consciousness can exist outside the brain. For now, let's look at what is typically reported to happen during a near death experience.

The Elements of Near Death Experiences

In December, 2008, I interviewed consciousness researcher Jody Long, who along with her husband, Jeffrey P. Long, M.D., founded the Near Death Experience Research Foundation. They maintain what they believe is the largest NDE web site (www.nderf.org) in the world. It has more than 1800 full-text published NDE accounts.

Five steps seem to be common to NDEs:

1. A sense of being dead, including the sudden awareness of a fatal accident, or of not surviving an operation.
2. An out-of-body experience; the sensation of peering down on one's body. As in the cases recounted above, those experiencing clinical death often report back the scene with uncanny accuracy, quoting doctors and witnesses verbatim.
3. Some kind of tunnel experience, a sense of moving upward or through a narrow passage.
4. Light, including light "beings," God or a Godlike entity. For having a hell-like experience, the opposite may be true—darkness or a lack of light.
5. A life review—being shown one's life, sometimes highlighting mistakes or omissions.

I find the life review of particular significance, and it never fails to come to mind whenever I'm tempted to do something that potentially might harm another. Here is what Raymond Moody, M.D., author of *Life After Life* and other books on this subject had to say about the life review:

When the life review occurs, there are no more physical surroundings. In their place is a full color, three-dimensional, panoramic review of every single thing the [persons having this experience] have done in their lives.

This usually takes place in a third-person perspective and doesn't occur in time as we know it. The closest description I've heard of it is that the person's whole life is there at once.

In this situation, you not only see every action that you have ever done, but you also perceive immediately the effect of every single one of your actions upon the people in your life.

So for instance, if I see myself doing an unloving act, then immediately I am in the consciousness of the person I did that act to, so that I feel their sadness, hurt, and regret.

On the other hand, if I do a loving act to someone, then I am immediately in their place and I can feel the kind and happy feelings.

Through all of this, the Being is with those people, asking them what good they have done with their lives. He helps them through this review and helps them put all the events of their life in perspective.

All of the people who go through this come away believing that the most important thing in their life is love.

Life After Death

For most of them, the second most important thing in life is knowledge. As they see life scenes in which they are learning things, the Being points out that one of the things they can take with them at death is knowledge. The other is love.

Chapter Three
Awareness Is Non Local

Back in the early 1930s a university with a new name and big ambitions hired a couple of men who wanted to unravel the mysteries of the paranormal. That university was Duke, located in Durham, North Carolina, now one of the most prestigious in the United States. The men were William McDougall and Joseph Banks Rhine, most often referred to as J. B. Rhine. The organization they created was called the Duke Parapsychology Laboratory for many years. Today it is called The Rhine Research Center, and although it is no longer connected with the University, it is located adjacent to the Duke campus.

What motivated these men? They wanted most to prove or disprove the fact or fiction of life after death. On my radio show that aired the week of April 6, 2009, I interviewed journalist Stacy Horn who wrote a book chronicling the history of this organization from 1930 to 1960, including experiments that were conducted and the interaction of the many people over the years. This included such well-known celebrities Upton Sinclair and scientists such as Albert Einstein. The name of her book is *UNBELIEVABLE: Investigations into Ghosts, Poltergeists, Telepathy, and Other Unseen Phenomena,* from the Duke Parapsychology Laboratory (HarperCollins, ECCO Imprint, 2009). Stacy went into this project a skeptic about paranormal phenomena, but was no longer a skeptic when she came out of it.

Previously known as Trinity College, a grant by tobacco millionaire James B. Duke in 1924 prompted the name change. Perhaps, the newly reconstituted school was looking for ways to make its mark when it lured William McDougall from Harvard University to set up a department of psychology.

He was soon contacted by a man named John Thomas who had 800 pages of transcripts generated by mediums he had been working with. Thomas' wife had died unexpectedly during an operation, and Thomas had been devastated. He began working with mediums in order to communicate with her.

Thomas got exciting results, but he wasn't sure he could believe them. Looking for verification of their authenticity, he traveled around the United States talking with mediums. He went to Europe, eventually, reasoning that mediums there would have no way of knowing anything about him or his wife. If they were able to come up with information that was accurate, it would be more convincing.

Ultimately, Thomas wrote to McDougall asking if he could send J. B. Rhine, then of Harvard University, and Rhine's wife Louisa, to Duke to study this material. McDougall agreed and Rhine came to Duke.

J. B. Rhine Takes Up Residence at Duke

Rhine studied Thomas' transcripts. He was able to verify

much of the information, and to all but eliminate fraud and lucky guesses. He traveled to Upstate New York, for example, investigating cemetery head stones to check out the veracity of genealogy of Thomas' wife indicated by a medium. The genealogy proved to be accurate. Not even Thomas himself knew if this genealogy was correct, but the information did check out. Ultimately, however, Rhine concluded that even though the information was correct, it could not be said with absolute certainty that the information was coming from Thomas' deceased, and now disembodied, wife.

The problem still dogs researchers who study the purported abilities of mediums. Assuming no fraud is being perpetrated, several possibilities exist as to the source of information coming from mediums that seems to be from a deceased individual:

1. It may actually be coming from the now disembodied individual.
2. The medium may be employing ESP or telepathy to read the minds of living individuals—in this case Thomas himself, or other living relatives of his wife. Indeed, a whole range of psychic abilities may be put to use including remote viewing, psychometry and clairvoyance. Nowadays, the full breadth of psychic abilities that might be at work is called "superpsi."
3. A third possibility is that the medium might be tapping into a reservoir of information of human history,

thoughts and feelings many believe exists. Some call this the Akashic Records, which are envisioned as the memory hard drive of the universe. The famous psychiatrist, Carl Jung, for example, wrote of a universal unconscious that holds the history and thoughts of all mankind. Today, researchers call this the "psychic reservoir." This is thought to be the source of information for perhaps most famous and well-documented psychic of the twentieth century, Edgar Cayce (1877-1945), often referred to as "The Sleeping Prophet"—Cayce became known as such because his readings were given while in a self-induced trance.

Rhine could find no way to prove superpsi, or the psychic reservoir, were not the source of information tapped into by mediums that had supposedly been in touch with Thomas' wife. So Rhine began putting his energy into the study of what became known as extra sensory perception, or ESP. He reasoned that if he could prove awareness extends beyond, and exists outside the body, a major step would be taken toward establishing the possibility of survival of consciousness after death. After all, for our consciousness to continue after death it has to be capable of existing outside the body and the brain. This chapter will establish this.

Conclusive Proof ESP

Rhine's most famous experiment used what has become known as ESP cards. Developed specifically for this purpose, these had different symbols on them including a star, wavy lines, a cross, a box and a circle. Many of these experiments were conducted—mostly using Duke University students—to see if people could tell what symbols were on the cards without looking at them. It was found again and again that they could.

The controls employed in these experiments were refined over time until neither the students nor those testing them could see one another. Ultimately, research was conducted in such a way that not even the person conducting the experiment knew what symbol was on the card a student was to identify. The experiments turned up statistically significant results time after time, showing without a doubt ESP is real.

One of Rhine's subjects in the ESP experiments was particularly impressive. A divinity student, his name was Hubert Pierce. Rhine believed that everyone possessed psychic abilities, but his research indicates some people have more talent for it than others. This is of course true of other abilities. An extremely talented singer will wow the judges and go on to win American Idol, but most will fail miserably and get the boot at the first audition.

There were twenty-five cards in the ESP deck, and five different symbols. Therefore, one would expect to guess five correctly each time through, simply by chance. Hubert Pierce could consistently get more than five correct, as could a number of others. But the interesting thing is, and according to Stacy Horn this came up frequently in the research, emotions played a role. Hubert, for example, needed money. He was a poor, struggling college student. Rhine once told him if he got the next card right, he'd pay him a hundred dollars. Pierce got it right. Rhine said, "Okay, get the next one right, and you'll get another hundred dollars."

Pierce got the next one right.

This went on through the entire deck. Pierce named all 25 cards correctly.

At one point, however, Hubert said he would not be coming into the lab for tests. His girlfriend had broken up with him, and he was heartbroken.

When he finally did come back, he did not perform well.

Another example of emotions playing a roll was the time Rhine tested the psychic abilities of children at a orphanage. One little girl became quite attached to a woman researcher. The little girl performed extremely well, apparently because she was eager to please, and wanted to prolong the session.

The Phenomenon of Remote Viewing

Something that demonstrates awareness is not local, but rather is non-local—at no particular place but everywhere at once—is the phenomenon of remote viewing. Those adept at remote viewing can direct their consciousness to be anywhere they want it to be.

Remote viewers use psychic powers to observe what's happening at a location some distance from them—in terms both of miles and in some cases, time as well.

Back in the 1970s, the U. S. government learned that the KGB was using psychics to spy on the United States. Naturally, U.S. Intelligence leaders wanted to see if this actually worked.

Did it? U.S. Army Major General Edmund R. Thompson, who was deputy Director for the Management and Operations for Defense Intelligence from 1982-84 is quoted as having said, "I never liked to get into debates with the skeptics, because if you didn't believe that remote viewing was real, you hadn't done your homework."

Remote viewing was used from the early 1970s forward through the Cold War to keep tabs on what the Soviets and Eastern Block countries were up to that couldn't be observed by spy planes, or satellites, or operatives on the ground.

In Spring 2009, I interviewed F. Holmes Atwater, the man who in 1979 set up the U.S. Army Intelligence unit responsible called Stargate. His friends know him by the name of Skip.

Skip got into this line of work through a series of what some people might call amazing coincidences, and others would say are synchronicities—events that look like coincidences, but seem to happen for a reason.

Skip grew up in a home with parents that took such things

for granted. It was the sort of thing they talked about at the dinner table. As a kid, Skip would go off on out-of-body trips almost nightly. He related one specific story to me and my listeners to illustrate this. He was seven or eight years old at the time, and it had to do with a problem he had with bedwetting.

"It was embarrassing," he said. "I had a big, brown piece of rubber on my bed so I wouldn't ruin the mattress. My parents didn't scold me, but they did make me responsible for washing my own sheets.

"I can remember distinctly waking up one night, and I was all wet. I was screaming in anger, and my mother came in and said, 'What's wrong? Did you fall out of bed?'

"I said, 'No, I remember, I got up, and I went down the hall to the bathroom, and I sat down. And the minute I started to pee, I woke up here in bed, and I'm all wet.'

"I was mad as the dickens, and my mother hugged me and said, 'Oh, that's all right, don't worry about it. You know, Skip, sometimes you're in your body and sometimes you're out of your body, and you have to remember that when you're going to the bathroom, make sure you're in your body.'

"[What she said] made perfect sense to me, and I said, 'Oh, now I understand,' and that was the end of my bedwetting."

Atwater Learns of Remote Viewing

Skip was in Army working for Army Intelligence when he came across a book called Mind Reach by Russell Targ and Harold E. Puthoff of the Stanford Research Institute. The book explained remote viewing, which didn't seem at all unusual to Skip given his experiences as a child. Naturally, a person could see things at a distance, using his mental powers. It was as though a light had suddenly flicked on. He instantly realized this could be used to gather intelligence.

At the time, Skip was in counter intelligence. It was his job to defend against wiretaps, bugging devices, and other forms of intelligence gathering by the enemy. No one in his counter intelligence unit had thought about remote viewing as a way the enemy might be spying on us. So Skip went to his commanding officer, a Colonel Webb, and gave him the book. After the Colonel had read it, Skip asked him if this remote viewing was being used on our side.

The Colonel had no idea. He thought if anything was going on, the Pentagon would be the place to find out. So he had Skip transferred to the Pentagon to take a position where he'd be in charge of a counter intelligence team. Skip would have the access he needed to find out about remote viewing and what if anything was being done about it to prevent the enemy from using it.

Before Skip was able to relocate to Washington, however, he received a change of orders. He was told to report to Fort Meade in Maryland. This was a better location for a young Army officer with a wife and children, which Skip had, because Fort Meade had family housing and good schools. It would be a much more affordable and pleasant place to live than Washington, D.C.

Documents Reveal U. S. Interest in Remote Viewing

At Fort Meade, Skip was assigned to what was known as a SAVE team—Security Activity Vulnerability Estimate team. The job was to go to sensitive U.S. installations and try to penetrate them in any way possible—as the enemy might in order to gather intelligence. Then the team would make a report to the commanding officer and provide recommendations for improving security.

Skip moved into his new job and was assigned an office that had just been vacated. The file cabinet and most of the desk drawers had been cleaned out, and an office safe had been emptied, but he did come across three documents in a bottom drawer of the desk that turned out to be classified. They reported on remote viewing experiments taking place in the Soviet sphere, funded by the KGB.

Skip took the documents to his supervising officer, a Major Keenan.

The Major looked at them. "Oh, yes, I remember these," he said. "The Lt. Colonel was very interested in this subject. Do you know anything about it?"

"Why, yes, I do, Major."

The Major took a moment and sized up Skip. "Lieutenant," he said, "from now on you're in charge of it."

And that's how Skip got his wish and started on a ten year career that eventually put him in charge of a remote viewing unit of the Army.

Atwater Learns about Remote Viewing

Skip soon learned that basic research had been underway since 1972 to check the validity of the Eastern Block experiments. The initial question had been whether reports of success were valid. It might be the Soviets were falsifying the results to create fear. The Stanford Research Institute had been retained to replicate the experiments paid for by the KGB. To the surprise of our intelligence community, the results had been positive.

By the time Skip got involved, the CIA and other U.S. intelligence agencies had been using natural psychics for some time to gather information, including well-known psychics such as Ingo Swann, who has since written several books on remote viewing. Skip's job became to set up, recruit and train remote viewers for U.S. Army Intelligence who may or not have had prior experience using psychic abilities. He developed a screening process, and for those who made the cut, a training program employing methodologies gleaned from accomplished remote viewers.

Skip's efforts met with success, but after a while he began looking for ways to enhance the results his remote viewers were achieving. This led him to The Monroe Institute (TMI) in Virginia, where he now works as Research Director.

The Monroe Institute Proves to Be a Resource

Robert Monroe (1915–1995) had spent a career in broadcasting, culminating as a vice president of NBC Radio. After leaving NBC, Monroe became known for his research into altered states of consciousness. His 1971 book Journeys Out of the Body is said to have popularized the term "out-of-body experience," or OBE.

Monroe's original objective had been to develop a process by which people could learn effortlessly—while they were asleep. He developed sound patterns that would help people reach a state called Stage Two Sleep and hold them in that state. Monroe experimented on himself and exposed himself to many varieties of sound. One night in 1956, quite unexpectedly, he found himself floating over his body. He panicked and thought the must be dying. He consulted medical doctors and psychiatrists about this, and eventually understood he wasn't dying—that this experience was fairly common. As a result, he conducted more experiments to learn how to replicate what he had done, and to control it.

By the time Monroe came to Skip's attention, he had established The Monroe Institute southwest of Charlottesville, Virginia, where the public could come to share in these sound-created experiences. Skip decided to investigate, and traveled from Fort Meade to Virginia to meet Monroe.

Skip, of course, was running a secret program for the U.S. Army and could not disclose the real reason for his visit. But he did explain to Monroe that he was interested in the work being done, had read his book, and had had out-of-body experiences as a child.

Monroe invited Skip to come into his laboratory. He took him to a room that had been set up and equipped for his experiments. He had Skip lie down. Skip became nervous. He was, after all, an intelligence officer on a surreptitious mission.

"What are these sounds I've heard about—these hemi-sync® sounds?" Skip asked.

"Oh, nothing to worry about," Monroe said. "I'll just play some music at first to calm you down."

As soon as Skip was lying down on the bed with the headphones on, the door shut and the lights went out. He wondered what he'd gotten himself into.

Music came through the speakers. It turned into the sound of surf against the shore. This reminded Skip of happy childhood days spent playing at the beach.

Then droning sounds came on in the background and quite unexpectedly the bed began to rise off the floor as though it were being lifted by hydraulics the way a car in a service station is lifted for an oil change.

Skip thought, Wow, this is a very special bed. They must have one of those lifts underneath it to push it up in the air.

As he was thinking about what must have been done to build it—the building had to have been constructed around it—he began to feel himself moving in a different direction. He seemed to be headed laterally, rather than up. That's when he realized it must not be a lift he was on. Yet the feeling was very strong, quite visceral, as though he were on an airplane circling into a landing approach. He saw or imagined that he was moving through a rock or crystal tunnel of some kind. Then he heard a voice.

"Whoa, there. What's happening, kid?" It was Robert Monroe.

"Well, I seem to be going some place," Skip said.

"Well, now, where're you going, kid?"

"I don't know," Skip answered.

Skip traveled along the tunnel, or corridor, and eventually came out of it in vast, open, white space. He said it was a little like being in a white cloud except there was no mist or fog. Everything was white, boundless, and there were no walls.

Perhaps the strangest part was that Skip watched himself arrive.

He thought, Gosh, I've come all this way only to find I'm already here.

Skip said in our interview, "It sounds trite to say wherever you go, there you are, but that's exactly what happened to me."

He remained in the white space for a while. Then he heard Robert Monroe's voice again:

"What's happening?"

Skip was embarrassed because he'd forgotten he was in Monroe's laboratory lying on a bed.

He said, "Oh, nothing much."

"Okay . . . well, it's time for lunch."

This didn't make sense, but that didn't matter because Monroe changed the sounds coming through the headphones, and

Skip felt the bed being lowered down to its original position. In a short time, the door was open and the lights were on.

Monroe was standing in the doorway.

Skip leaned over and looked under the bed.

"Oh, did you lose your wallet down there?" Monroe asked.

Skip was looking for the hydraulic lift, but there was none.

As a result of this experience, he learned there was definitely something to the sound technology Robert Monroe had developed, and the Army entered into a classified contract with Robert Monroe to do some training.

The Amazing Abilities of Joe McMoneagle

One man Monroe trained was perhaps the most outstanding remote viewer in the Army. His name is Joe McMoneagle.

Joe had been in intelligence before joining Skip's unit. His personal story is fascinating and was related to me by a guest on my show who'd gotten to know Joe over the years through an association with The Monroe Institute.

In the early 1970s, Joe was the target of a successful assassination attempt while in the Army stationed in Germany, working as an operative in intelligence. Poison was the method. He was meeting with an intelligence contact at a restaurant, having dinner, when he felt nauseous. He excused himself and went outside to get some air. He walked around for a moment, and then saw a crowd gathered just outside the door. He went to see what the commotion was about, looked through the crowd, and could make out a body laying on the street.

People were saying, "He's dead, he's dead!"

Joe came closer and was shocked to see the body was his own.

Testing later showed he'd been subjected to a binary poison, one which becomes toxic when combined with another substance. This had allowed his assassin to slip him the poison and make his getaway before Joe sat down to dinner and consumed whatever had triggered the toxicity that killed him.

McMoneagle's consciousness, after viewing his body lying on the street, went toward the light and through the tunnel described by Pam Reynolds and other near-death survivors. As is now considered typical in these cases, he arrived at a place where he was met by spiritual beings. There, he underwent some instruction and a life review. We would know nothing of this if Joe's body had not been resuscitated. His recovery and recuperation took quite some time.

What happened that evening changed Joe in several ways. He'd had psychic experiences before his NDE, but had kept them to himself. He no longer did. He also began to have spontaneous out-of-body experiences he was unable to control.

Joe's case came to the attention of two physicists at the Stanford Research Institute, Russell Targ and Harold Puthoff. They'd already been working on a government contract to study the ramifications of the quantum mechanics theory of non locality of consciousness. These were the same experiments described in the classified document found by Skip Atwater, and the same two men who'd authored the book he'd read.

Joe became the first remote viewer directly on the government payroll. In the course of his career in the Army as a remote viewer, Joe worked on more than 200 missions, many of which were reported at the highest levels of the U.S. military and government. Some of the information was considered so crucial, vital and unavailable from any other source, that he was awarded the Legion of Merit for his work, the second highest award the Army can give to someone in the military during peacetime.

Skylab's Fall to Earth Is Accurately Predicted

One such mission was to determine the time and the location Skylab would fall to earth. Depending on how old you are, you may recall Skylab—literally a scientific laboratory in orbit around the earth, put there for astronauts to conduct experiments in space. Launched in 1973, it weighed about 100 tons.

By 1979 its orbit was decaying and Skylab was expected to come down. The question was, "Where?"

A hundred ton metal object falling on a heavily populated area such as New York, Tokyo or London, for example, would cause a tremendous death and destruction. Super computers were enlisted to answer the question, but too many variables existed for the technology of the day. The results were unreliable.

Joe McMoneagle, Ingo Swann and a third individual, a woman whose name I have been unable to uncover, were contracted with individually to come up with an answer. None of the three knew the others were involved. All picked the same day, July 11, 1979, and almost the same time. Each was within five minutes of the other two. This was nine and a half months before Skylab came down. In addition, they all picked a location in western Australia within five miles of one another—a remote, uninhabited area.

Skylab came down there, all right, almost precisely as predicted, demonstrating awareness is not located just inside our skulls, nor is it limited in time and space—more evidence my one-mind theory is correct.

The Capture of Saddam Hussein Is Seen Six Weeks Ahead

Another startling example that awareness is non local comes from a book by Stephan A. Schwartz, *OPENING TO THE INFINITE: The Art and Science of Nonlocal Awareness* (Nemoseen Media, 2007). Mr. Schwartz was on my radio show in the summer of 2008. One of the amazing stories he told was about the predictions made by a college seminar class about the capture of Saddam Hussein. On November 2, 2003, after being taught the basic skills of remote viewing, 47 of those who'd attended the seminar agreed to "Describe the location of Saddam Hussein at the time of this capture or discovery by U.S. or coalition forces." The students' data was collected and analyzed, including points of consensus concerning the physical location, as well as things that were not likely to be predictable—such as Hussein's appearance on the day of his capture. The data were photocopied and distributed to a number of people, and then turned over to a third party, Herk Stokeley, Director of Atlantic University. Stokeley placed the data in an envelope, which he sealed in front of a notary, who affixed her seal across the envelope's flap. The envelope was then placed in a vault.

Hussein was captured about six weeks later, on December 13, 2003. The remote viewing documents in the safe said he would be beneath an ordinary looking house on the outskirts of a small village near the city of Tikrit, and that the house would be part of a small compound that's bordered on one side by a dirt road and, on the other by a nearby river. Two large palm trees would mark the ends of the house. All this turned out to be true.

Remote viewing also predicted Hussein would be found crouching in a subterranean room or cave reached by a tunnel. This was true.

Remote viewing said Hussein would look like a homeless person with dirty rough clothing, long ratty hair and a substantial and equally ratty salt and pepper beard. This was true.

Remote viewing said he would have only two or three supporters with him at the time of his discovery. He had two.

Remote viewing said he'd have a gun with him. He had a pistol.

Remote viewing said he would have a quantity of money. He had $750,000 in cash.

Remote viewing said he would be defiant, but would not put up any resistance and would be tired and dispirited. This was true.

What's the take-away from all this? The one mind we all share contains all—past, present and future.

Chapter Four
Proof of Accurate Information about the Dead

One scientist has proven beyond the shadow of a doubt it's possible for bona fide mediums to relate accurate and specific information about deceased individuals to living loved ones under blinded conditions—without the use fraud, visual or verbal clues, or any other possible deceit or deception. Her name is Julie Beischel, and she has a Ph.D. in pharmacology and toxicology. This may be an unusual background for a paranormal researcher, but it may also be the reason she has been able to come up with an airtight methodology that proves mediums can do what they have long claimed to be able to do. A big part of what pharmacologists do is determine the efficacy, or lack there of, of drugs. Doing so requires constructing foolproof, double blind experiments.

I met with Dr. Beischel during a lunch break at the Society for Scientific Exploration's Annual Meeting in May 2009, at the University of Virginia in Charlottesville. We talked for more than an hour. A few weeks later she also was a guest on my radio show, and I was able to ask follow up questions.

Dr. Beischel received her Ph.D. from the University of Arizona at a time something occurred to prompt her to change her career direction.

Her mother committed suicide.

The Author's Wish to Communicate with His Father

Out of a sense of propriety, I did not ask Dr. Beischel how she felt about her mother's suicide, and what questions it may have raised, but I can imagine how I would have felt had it happened in my family. The suicide of a parent must certainly be one of the most devastating events that can occur. I can imagine this because my father died when I was seven years old. He didn't commit suicide—he died of a heart attack. Nevertheless, I went through much of my life—well into adulthood—wondering if I had been the cause. The day before the night he died he'd become very angry with me. Looking back, I don't recall specifically what I did to set him off. Perhaps, I'd made a big mess in the kitchen, or written on a wall with pen or pencil. I must have done something children do to create a mess an adult has to clean up. Whatever it may have been, I can still recall how red in the face he became.

That was the last time I saw him, alive.

I assumed I'd been responsible for bringing on the heart attack that killed him. Now, with four kids of my own who have created their share of messes over the years, I can rationalize that idea away.

His life style did him in. He ate too much, and he smoked. He never exercised and he had grown a potbelly in just a couple of years. Maybe he had an unconscious death wish—who knows? Whatever the case, I now see he was a heart attack waiting to happen. But, at the age of seven, I wasn't worldly wise enough to figure that out. Suffice it to say, the question haunted me for years, "Had I caused my father's death?"

Now, think about this. Suppose I'd been able to ask a medium and get an answer—an answer I could be confident was true? Imagine how much worry and anxiety that would have saved me.

Know what? Now, thanks to Dr. Beischel, others in such a situation can do just that.

I don't know what questions Dr. Beischel may have had for her mother, but she must have had some. A basic one likely was, "Does my mother's consciousness still exist?"

Dr. Beischel told me science is her religion. Quite naturally, that's where she turned for the answer.

She wanted to know what science could tell her about life after death. "Very little," was the answer.

As fate would have it, Dr. Gary Schwartz at the University of Arizona was conducting a good deal of what little research was being done on this subject—precisely where Dr. Beischel happened to be at the time.

From Pharmacology to Consciousness Research

A book by Schwartz detailing his work with mediums was published in 2002 by Atria Books called, *THE AFTERLIFE EXPERIMENTS: Breakthrough Scientific Evidence of Life After Death*. I understand Dr. Schwartz has been subjected to a good deal of criticism from skeptics about this research. They claim his methodologies were riddled with holes. Finding a spot for Dr. Beischel in his research laboratory no doubt made a lot of sense because she was trained to come up with methodologies no one could poke holes in. For the next couple of years she worked closely with him.

When I spoke with Dr. Beischel, I asked about Dr. Schwartz's work that turned out to have been done before she joined him. She couldn't talk about that, of course, except to say when she came on board she felt more stringent controls were needed. In 2007 when Schwartz's research turned in a different direction, Dr. Beischel and her husband, Mark Boccuzzi—who'd been researching hauntings—founded the Windbridge Institute for Applied Research in Human Potential.

Windbridge seems to have captured almost instant credibility in the paranormal research field. The Advisory Board reads like a who's who of respected paranormal researchers. It includes a couple whose work is reported upon in this book—Jim B. Tucker, M.D., of the University of Virginia who is researching children's memories of past lives, and Stephen Braude, Ph.D., of the University of Maryland Baltimore County who as been researching the paranormal for more than 30 years, and has written a number of books on the subject.

Airtight Methodology Is Developed

Dr. Beischel developed a methodology no one can question to test the abilities of mediums who claim to communicate with the dead. The screening process she developed takes about a year to complete. Those who pass it are certified by Windbridge, and their contact information is given on www.windbridge.com. So, if you have questions for a deceased loved one—as I did way back when—you now have a place you can go that you can feel good about.

Each prospective Windbridge medium is screened using an intensive eight-step screening and training procedure:

Step 1: Written Questionnaire
Step 2: Personality/Psychological Tests
Step 3: Phone Interview with an existing WCRM
Step 4: Phone Interview with a Windbridge Investigator
Step 5: Two Blinded Phone Readings
Step 6: Mediumship Research Training
Step 7: Human Research Subjects Training
Step 8: Grief Training

Upon successful completion of the eight steps, the medium becomes a Level One Windbridge Certified Research Medium (WCRM-1). The mediums' certification levels increase over time, from Level 1 to Level 5, as they participate in additional research studies.

Each WCRM agrees to donate a minimum of four hours per month to assist in various aspects of the research, to uphold a code of spiritual ethics, to embrace a strong commitment to the values of scientific mediumship research, and to abide by specific Windbridge standards of conduct.

Life After Death

Before we discuss Dr. Beischel's mediumship research, let me define some terms. A "discarnate" is a dead person with whom the medium supposedly communicates. A "sitter" is the loved one of the discarnate for whom the reading is done. A "proxy sitter" is someone who asks the questions in place of the sitter, and knows nothing about the discarnate.

The procedure is as follows. Two different, unrelated individuals are selected who would like to contact deceased loved ones. Questions are developed for the discarnates. These include such specifics as a physical description, cause of death, and the discarnate's hobbies during life. The discarnates involved must be the same sex but have different physical descriptions, occupations in life, ages and manners of death. No confusion should be possible if medium's answers are correct.

Dates and times are set for the readings, usually on separate days.

Sitters aren't told the times or dates of readings but are asked to request that the deceased loved one communicate with the right medium at the right time.

A proxy sitter who has no knowledge of the discarnates except for their first names, contacts the medium by telephone on the prescribed date and time for each reading.

Let's say the discarnates are Suzie and Betty. The session asking the medium questions for Suzie is recorded and, later, transcribed.

On the day and time of the next reading, the questions for Betty are asked. This session is also recorded and transcribed.

In both cases, ambiguous answers are adjusted so that they lack ambiguity. For example, if the medium says Suzie's hair color was reddish, the answer is changed to "red."

Following these sessions, both sitters are given both sets of answers—without names on them. They are asked to score each item for accuracy and then rate the reports over on a scale of one to six based on how strongly they portray the loved one who was to be contacted.

This procedure eliminates the possibility of fraud. All the proxy sitter and medium have is a first name, making it impossible to find out anything about the person through conventional means. The medium cannot give answers based on visual or verbal clues because a proxy sitter who knows nothing about the discarnate asks the questions. In addition, the session is conducted by telephone.

Rater bias is also eliminated. The sitter does not know which answer sheet is for his or her loved one, and which is not.

The argument is eliminated that the answers are too general or are being judged as accurate based on wishful thinking on part of sitter because the answers deal in specifics—physical description, occupation, manner of death and so forth.

Dr. Beischel told me that discarnates often find ingenious ways to communicate their presence and survival to a loved one. In one example, the discarnate communicated to the medium about a white car the medium herself had purchased on Halloween and nicknamed "Casper"—for the friendly cartoon ghost. When asked why the discarnate might have done so, the sitter said, "Well, I suppose it's because our last name is Kasperi."

Statistically Significant Results

The results of this research have been highly significant, statistically. On a scale of one to six—with one being not at all accurate, and six extremely accurate—the average score is about 3.5 for readings containing the loved one's answers, and less than 2.0 for the control readings. That's a sizable difference.

The scores just stated are of compilations of many readings averaged together. Some scores are considerably higher and some lower, including low scores in which the discarnate may have decided not to participate. PDFs of peer reviewed papers giving all the details can be downloaded for review by anyone interested at the Windbridge web site, www.Windbridge.org.

Dr. Beischel told me that after a research session is done, sitters often contact the mediums directly for a follow up session. Follow up sessions normally produce accuracy scores in the neighborhood of 85 to 90 percent.

The most obvious explanation for the findings of this research is that human consciousness continues after death. This is supported by research being conducted at the University of Virginia by Jim B. Tucker, M.D., that will be covered later, and by the Pam Reynolds and Kristle Merzlock near death case histories recounted in Chapter Two. It is also supported by the experiences of the mediums themselves. All consistently report a difference between a session communicating with a discarnate, and what is called a psychic reading, which is done for a living person. They typically feel a presence when dealing with a discarnate.

How You Can Contact a Deceased Loved One

If you are wondering about a deceased loved one or have questions you'd like him or her to answer, you might consider having a reading done. Simply go to the Windbridge.org home page and click on "Research Mediums." You'll find an alphabetical listing of certified mediums along with their contact information.

The Ghost of Philippe Sirot

As mentioned above, mediums consistently report they feel a presence when doing a discarnate reading. They say they feel no such presence when doing a psychic reading for a living person. This has been described by one medium as the difference between "watching a play and reading a book."

Anyone who has experienced such a presence will know what the mediums mean by "presence." Some years ago I experienced the presence of a deceased friend named Philippe, who had been engaged to one of my first wife's good friends named Joel. It happened at Joel's house in Marseilles, France.

The house where she lived with her mother was situated on a steep, curved lane where walls hid quiet gardens, on the southern side of the hill below the Cathedral of Notre Dame, which is topped by a statue of the holy Madonna. This icon of the mother of Jesus looks down from the highest point in that city. She has a magnificent view of the burning bright, azure harbor and the island fortress of Count of Monte Cristo fame. The house was a hundred feet or so directly below Mary's statue, behind an iron gate, recessed into the side of the hill. The stucco covered stone house had three levels, the bottom of which was an English basement at grade with a terrace. This had been turned into a separate apartment and rented out.

The first tenant turned out to be a dashing young man who worked with Jacques Cousteau (1910–1997). This young Frenchman, Philippe Sirot, gallivanted around the world on a converted minesweeper called the Calypso along with Cousteau and his motley ban of adventurers and marine biologists. The apartment in the quiet Marseilles neighborhood was where he lived when he wasn't gallivanting. As luck and love would have it, he and Joel fell for each other and got engaged. My first wife and I had chummed around with them before my wife and I were married, and when we two tied the knot, Philippe had been the French equivalent of my best man. She had been the maid of honor.

Life After Death

That had been in happier times. The mood was somber when we arrived at the house in Marseilles that year. Only a few months prior, the dashing young man had died a tragic death.

Philippe had been possessed of a fascination with death. He sincerely believed that it did not represent the end. Rather, he hypothesized that we enter another dimension, that we "cross over" into what I now realize is the mental world of spirit that in many respects mirrors the physical side of existence. Looking back with the perspective that time and increased knowledge give, I believe his preoccupation, his burning curiosity, may have led him to harbor an unconscious death wish. I recall vividly how he would barrel down a narrow Marseilles city street on a 750 cc Triumph motorcycle at 120 miles an hour. He did this once with me hanging on in back. You cannot imagine the sheer terror I felt at the time. He also flew small planes, once taking a Piper Cub to Corsica across open water at night with no instruments.

Skydiving was another hobby, and deep sea diving was part of his job. You can still catch sight of Philippe on television, in reruns of *The Undersea World of Jacques Cousteau,* playing ring around the rosy with a bunch of hungry sharks.

Philippe Falls into Despair

In the year or two leading up to our visit to Marseilles that year, Philippe had fallen into despair, and his death was thought to have been the result of suicide.

Several things had gone wrong for him. First, by that time—the mid 1970s—Cousteau and the Calypso were no longer taking voyages to exotic locations. Replacing a job as a seafaring adventurer isn't easy. But he needed one, and he'd taken a position as captain of a boat that tended offshore oil-rigs. The result was that he was bored to death, perhaps almost literally.

Second, his romance with Joel was on the rocks. From what I could determine, they'd broken up after a couple of silly arguments. She was still mad about him, but was playing a game some people play—hard to get. She refused to see him, no matter how he tried.

Who knows what else had gone wrong. Other factors may have come into play that I cannot recall or of which I was unaware. But the bottom line was, he was found dead one day in his cabin at sea.

Philippe Promises to Communicate with His Friends

On several occasions Philippe had told friends that he would communicate with them after he died if it were possible. This occurred to me as I paid the cab driver and collected our luggage.

Joel was aflutter when we arrived. She was bursting to unload a lot of pent up stuff on my wife. For starters, her wristwatch had stopped when his funeral had begun, and had not resumed until the moment the funeral ended. I didn't see that this actually proved anything, but it did make me wonder. Anyway, I didn't have much opportunity to think because Joel was jabbering on and on about black cats and bumps in the night.

We all had a late dinner that evening, and I decided to turn in. My head was starting to ache from trying to keep up with the conversation, which was in French. It looked as though Joel and my wife were well on the way to staying up all night talking, so I suggested that I put our daughter Sophie to bed and then turn in myself.

Sophie was in another room, playing with her dolls. We said good night to her mom and Joel, descended a dark, circular staircase, and walked hand in hand through a dimly lit storage room. As in past years, we'd be sleeping in Philippe's old apartment. My hand closed around the knob and I pushed the door open.

Nothing had changed. Every piece of furniture, every wall hanging was exactly as he'd left it.

I Experience Philippe's Presence

The most bizarre sensation overwhelmed me. I felt that Philippe was there in the room, present among his belongings: the American Indian throw on the bed, the primitive masks and spears on the walls, the little statues and knickknacks from all over the world, including local deities and fertility gods. His presence was palpable, and it grew more so each second, seeming to close in on me, as if he had moved close to examine my face. I could almost feel his breath.

I did not want to upset my daughter, so I helped her into her pajamas, and went through the usual bedtime routine of a story. At last, I put her down in a child's bed, which had been positioned at the foot of Philippe's, and turned out the lights—except for one by the bed I'd use to read by. Then I crawled under the covers.

All was silent. I opened a book but could not concentrate. Philippe's presence was strong, particularly when I looked at the primitive wall hanging of a sunburst. The hand-woven image reminded me of the rising sun of Japan. My eyes were drawn to the center until the circle filled my vision.

What seemed a disembodied voice said, "Don't think about ghosts. It doesn't do any good to think about ghosts."

It was my daughter, Sophie. I'd thought she was asleep, but along with every hair on my body, she was sitting up.

I had no idea she even knew what a ghost was, or rather what a ghost was supposed to be. We'd never talked about them. At that point in my life, I wasn't sure they existed. I was still a materialist, not having come to the conclusion the world view I'd bought into was off base.

In retrospect I should have asked, "Why do you say that, dear?" But I wasn't thinking clearly. Instead, I said, "That's correct, dear. It doesn't do any good to think about ghosts." She laid down, and I didn't hear from her again that night.

What do you suppose caused her to sit up and make that rather interesting observation?

I have to wonder if Philippe wasn't fulfilling his promise and communicating with me through my three year old daughter's half-asleep mind. Anyhow, the sense of his presence was undeniable and prevents me from dismissing the reports of psychics of feeling a presence during a chat with a discarnate.

The need for the actual presence of a discarnate may also be the reason psychics aren't able to conjure up discussions with dead historical figures such as Abraham Lincoln, George Washington or Napoleon Bonaparte. What would be in it for them to show up? Why should they? To make the cover of the *National Enquirer?*

On the other hand, my dead father might have been perfectly willing to come to a séance that would have given him the opportunity to assure me it wasn't my scribbling on the kitchen wall with magic marker, and his resulting fit of anger, that led to his coronary thrombosis.

Or, maybe he'd say it was.

Time for a New Paradigm

As previously discussed, besides continuation of consciousness after death, there are two other possible explanations for psychics' ability to give accurate information about the dead: the possible tapping into of a psychic reservoir, and what paranormal researchers call superpsi—the combination of clairvoyance, telepathy, remote viewing and so forth. Dr. Beischel joked that the only way to disprove the superpsi hypothesis when studying mediums is if they are able to retrieve information that never has and never will exist in the physical universe.

No matter which of the three possible explanations is correct, as in the case of NDEs and remote viewing, none fit the paradigm currently accepted by the majority of mainstream scientists today—the paradigm some have labeled "materialistic-reductionist science." This paradigm holds that the only reliable knowledge about the nature of the physical universe is that gained by the five ordinary senses. It rejects the notion that anything can survive the death of the body and has led to the erroneous and devastatingly harmful view held by practitioners of modern psychology that the brain is the seat of consciousness. The idea of a nonmaterial mind or soul that can survive death is held to be impossible.

How science stumbled off onto the wrong track will be discussed, but first let me explain how Dr. Beischel intends to determine if continuation of consciousness or one of the other two possibilities accounts for how mediums can report accurate information about discarnates.

Research on Discarnate Vs. Living Person Readings

As mentioned, Dr. Beischel has gathered a good deal of qualitative as well as quantitative information concerning how mediums feel when they are conducting a reading with a discarnate—a presence; viewing a play—as opposed to how they feel while doing a reading for a living person, i.e., reading a book. She has published a peer-reviewed paper about this.

Next, she plans to develop a research methodology wherein the psychic will be asked to give two readings, one to gather information from a discarnate, and the other about a living person. The psychic will not know which is which. All he or she will be given is a first name. Data concerning the psychic's feelings about the reading and the person they are gathering information about will be collected to see if there is statistically significant support for what the mediums have been reporting.

Dr. Beischel Communicates with Her Mom

You may be wondering, as I did during that first interview, if Dr. Beischel was able to contact her mother through a medium. She said she was—that she did so once. She said the session convinced her the medium was not employing telepathy to read her [Julie's] mind. The medium was talking about a brown station wagon her mother used to drive. Immediately, Julie recalled as a child having left a green crayon in that station wagon that melted into the carpet because of the Arizona heat.

Her mind screamed, Green crayon! Green crayon!

But the medium never said anything about a green crayon. Perhaps the most convincing and certainly most dramatic contact with her deceased mother, however, was in the form of a dream. She had dreamed about her mother before, about seeing her with bags packed and leaving. That had been an ordinary dream. The convincing dream was one in which her mother spoke to her. It was vivid, lifelike and seemed absolutely real. I've had lucid dreams on occasion and I imagine that's what it was like. I did not ask the content of Dr. Beischel's dream, but apparently Julie got whatever answers she was looking for.

Communications with the Dead in the Dream State

The famous psychic Edgar Cayce, who gave more than 14,000 psychic readings, suggested a number of times that our loved ones who have passed away often try to communicate with us in the dream state. Dream researcher, Jody Long, who has been a guest on my radio show, believes being in the dream state may make it easier for loved ones who have passed to communicate with us. Our subconscious mind has its guard up in the waking state so that only a tiny amount of what is going on around us enters our consciousness. If this were not the case, we would simply be unable to process all the stimuli available to us. In the dream or drowsy state, however, our guard is down, lowering the threshold. This may make it easier to receive communications from the other side.

My apologies to regular listeners of my radio show who have heard me tell the story that follows, but I feel compelled to do so as it relates directly to receiving messages from the other side while in the dream or drowsy state. It has to do with an acquaintance of mine, a French count named Henri Dmitry. He told me this story about twenty-five years ago when my first wife and I were spending several days with him and his wife their chateau in Lorraine.

Henri had inherited his castle and the land and village around it along with his title—long after the castle had fallen into disrepair. It had not been lived in since before World War Two.

The Source of Night Noises Is Tracked Down

Having done well in business, Henri decided to restore the old place. He and his wife spend quite a bit of time there as it was undergoing renovation and were often disturbed in the middle of the night by what seemed to be someone down in the basement screaming. Inevitably, it would wake them up. At other times, they would hear the noise in that drowsy state as they were falling asleep or waking up. This happened almost every night. Finally, they became so annoyed, Henri had the workmen tear out a wall he judged to be the place from which the nocturnal uproar was emanating.

A skeleton was behind it.

Henri and his wife had no idea who the skeleton belonged to, but they gave it a Christian burial. Afterward, they were never again bothered by the night noises.

Here's what Henri thought about this. A man had been bricked up behind the wall while he was still alive—someone didn't like the guy. Maybe he'd been knocked on the head. Maybe he came to after the bricks were put in place. Then he died, but he did not realize it.

We will go into a full discussion of this phenomenon in an upcoming chapter. Suffice it to say the spirit of this dead person could easily have passed through the bricks, but the dead man didn't know this because he didn't know he was dead. He'd been calling for help ever since. Of course, these were psychic screams, since the ghost had no vocal cords. The middle of the night was the only time the screams for help penetrated the minds of Henri and his wife because that was when all else was quiet, and they were sleeping, or near sleep, and their minds were sensitive to such things.

The dead man didn't know how long he'd been trapped behind the bricks. People who have studied this sort of thing say time is not experienced in the spirit dimension. In an upcoming chapter we will learn why this is so.

Chapter Five
Evidence from the Past Consciousness Continues

In August, 2008, I interviewed Stephen Braude, Ph.D., Editor-in-Chief of the *Journal of Scientific Exploration* and at the time a professor of philosophy at the University of Maryland, Baltimore County. We talked about his book *IMMORTAL REMAINS: The Evidence for Life After Death.*

Dr. Braude has been researching the paranormal for more than 30 years. I was curious to know how he got interested.

He said he was in graduate school and a hard nosed materialist at the time. He'd never really thought about things psychic. A couple of friends came over one day, looking for something to do, and suggested the three of them play a game called "Table Up."

It turned out this meant, "Let's have a séance."

For the next three hours, Dr. Braude watched his table rise in the air and spell out the answers to questions posed by him and his friends. Dr. Braude said that typically in these sorts of sessions, yes or no questions are asked. The table is asked to tilt once for yes and twice for no. But he and his friends didn't know this and asked open ended questions, telling the table to tilt once for the letter A, twice for B, three times for C and so forth. As you can imagine, this got rather tedious.

This happened in broad daylight. It happened in Dr. Braude's house. And his table did the tilting.

He added that none of the three of them were stoned.

He and both his friends would sometimes stand next to the table to verify no one's knees were doing the lifting. The table would still rise under their fingers.

Dr. Braude's curiosity was aroused by this session, and he has been studying the paranormal ever since. This has led to many run ins with pseudo skeptics, which may be the reason he knows just about every possible argument to shoot down the idea that mediums can communicate with the dead.

Unlike Julie Beischel, Stephen Braude does not to my knowledge conduct original research. He delves into eyewitness accounts from reliable witnesses that come from the heyday of spiritualism—the late nineteen and early twentieth centuries. At that time, many mediums were "trance mediums," which means a discarnate would take over their bodies and speak through them, using a medium's voice box and vocal cords to speak. Mediums no longer do this. You will understand why, later, when we delve into the topic of spirit possession.

Factors Dr. Braude Uses to Judge Veracity of Claims

Professor Braude says he considers a number of factors to judge the veracity of reports of discarnates speaking through mediums. Some he calls the usual suspects: Mis-reporting, mal-observation, hidden memories, i.e., things people forgot about, or fraud. Then there are the unusual suspects: photographic memory, prodigies, idiot savants, and the remarkable things people can sometimes do when hypnotized.

But he doesn't stop there. Even if he finds a case that can't be explained by the usual or unusual suspects, that old bugaboo, psychic functioning among the living, otherwise known as superpsi, still looms. Obviously, people want to think their loved one survived and, when their time comes, they will survive death as well. Plus, the medium wants to satisfy a client. So what appears valid may simply be a good show put on by the medium, combined with a willing and credulous audience.

For this reason, he says the most convincing cases are those in which a discarnate drops into a séance and no one present knows the discarnate who has dropped in. This is especially true when the discarnate—communicating through the medium's voice box—does not give information that in any way supports or fulfills the needs or desires of anyone present. The most compelling are cases are when what the discarnate says makes sense only in terms of the discarnate's interests or agenda. For example, the discarnate may have unfinished business to take care of. Otherwise, why would he or she show up? Such cases do exist.

The Case of the Icelandic Drunkard

One related to me by Dr. Braude took place at a séance in Iceland. On several occasions, a trance medium's body was taken over by a "drop-in" discarnate with a drinking problem. The medium didn't drink, but that didn't stop the discarnate from repeatedly demanding alcohol while speaking through the medium's body to those present.

The discarnate gave information about himself that was later confirmed by a variety of sources. But most remarkable, he claimed to be looking for his leg.

First, he said his leg was in the sea. Then he said it was in the wall of a house belonging to one of those at the séance.

Later, research undertaken by the séance attendees found this man had been in a drunken stupor by the ocean, had fallen asleep, and was washed out to sea by the tide. His body eventually returned to shore, where it was torn to pieces by dogs and ravens.

Most of the man's bones were recovered and buried, but not all of them. The discarnate said a thighbone had not been buried and was in the wall of a house where one séance participant lived.

This participate later talked to the man who'd built his house and indeed found the builder had put a thighbone, a femur, in one wall. DNA testing did not exist back then so it wasn't possible to prove the femur actually belonged to the man. But the discarnate had been tall, and the femur in the wall had belonged to a tall man.

A Convincing Case of Reincarnation

When it comes to reincarnation, Dr. Braude has a keen eye for motives that might indicate fraud, and factors that seem to indicate superpsi or the psychic reservoir are not the sources of information. Among children who recall past lives, for example, this would include highly emotional reunions with relatives from the past life such as wives, husbands or children. He also looks for attitudes or knowledge that a child normally would not be expected to have.

He spoke of one convincing case—that of a young boy in India who claimed to be the reincarnation of a man who had lived quite some distance away. The man he claimed to have been had lived a life of debauchery and had carried on extensively with a prostitute. After his rebirth, and having achieved the ripe old age of three, he advised his father to get himself a mistress.

His father asked why.

The child replied that he would have much pleasure from her, and went into some detail about what he meant by pleasure—not the sort of thing one would expect to hear from a three year old.

Body Parts Contain Urges and Desires

Dr. Braude also talked about transplant cases. These are situations where a heart or kidneys or some other organ is transplanted and the recipient starts having feelings and cravings that seem to have belonged to the organ donor. This indicates the brain is not the only physical link to our desires and preferences. Dr. Braude told the story of a young man who received a heart-lung transplant from a lesbian painter. After his recovery from the surgery, his girlfriend reported that his personality had changed dramatically. He now enjoyed hanging out in art galleries, he seemed to have developed an understanding of and deep appreciation for landscape paintings, and perhaps most interesting, his lovemaking was completely different. He showed a definite appreciation and understanding of female anatomy that he had not possessed before.

The Little Lady Who Craved Chicken Nuggets & Beer

I learned of another case from a different source. After a heart transplant, a lady began having constant cravings for chicken nuggets and beer. This was odd because she'd never had chicken nuggets before, and she didn't drink beer or any other kind of alcoholic beverage—at least not before her surgery. After having a recurring dream in which a young man came to her saying he loved her and had given her his heart, she decided to find out who her new heart had come from. Following a good deal of detective work, she learned it had belonged to a young man, the victim of a motorcycle crash, who'd been found with a box of MacDonald's chicken nuggets and a six pack of beer stuffed inside his motorcycle jacket.

The Lumberjack Who Liked Housework & Knitting

Here's another case. Back on January 17, 2006—I know the date because I jotted it down—I took a lunch break from writing *A Witch in the Family,* a book about my ancestor, Susannah North Martin, who was hanged as a witch in Salem, Massachusetts, in 1692. While eating, I watched a series of online video clips at a news web site. One of these reported on a Croatian lumberjack who had received a lifesaving kidney transplant and now was suing the hospital that gave it to him. The man's favorite pastime had once been spending time in the local pub, carousing with his buddies. Now, he had developed a passion for housework and knitting. This had made him the laughing stock of his village. He believed the kidney was to blame, and he was probably right. The donor was a 51 year-old-woman.

I asked Dr. Braude what was the most convincing case he'd come across. He said it was that of Leonora Piper, who for many years consistently gave accurate readings to loved ones and to proxies of loved ones about discarnates.

The Case of Leonora Simonds Piper

Leonora Simonds Piper was born in Nashua, New Hampshire in June 1859. Her first inkling toward her future career occurred when she was only eight years-old, playing in the garden. She felt a sharp pain in her right ear and a whispered voice said, "Aunt Sara, not dead, but with you still."

Terrified, Leonora ran into the house and told her mother. They found out later her Aunt Sara had died at about the moment this had occurred.

Leonora's mediumship began in earnest in 1884 after her father-in-law took her for a medical consultation with J.R. Cook, a blind clairvoyant who had a reputation for diagnosing illnesses and suggesting cures. Leonora lost consciousness at Cook's touch and entered a trance. Later, she attended a home circle sitting, otherwise known as a seance, and entered a trance in which she produced a message for someone present. The person considered the message to be the most accurate he had received during his 30 year interest in Spiritualism.

It wasn't long before Leonora began giving private seances in her home. This is how she became acquainted with Professor William James of Harvard, a founder of the Pragmatic School of Thought, which held that only those principles that can be demonstrated—not only theoretically but practically—deserve intelligent consideration. Even though he was an unbending pragmatist, Leonora converted him to a belief in psychic phenomena to such a degree that he became one of the founding members of the American Society for Psychical Research (ASPR).

Leonora came to Professor James' attention through his mother-in-law, a Mrs. Gibbens, who heard about her through friends and decided to schedule an appointment. After her meeting with Piper, she returned to the James' home and told the professor that in a trance, Piper had told her facts about relatives, living and dead, she could not have possibly have known in any normal way. James laughed and called Mrs. Gibbens a "victim" of a medium's trickery. He gave her an explanation as to how mediums accomplished their fraud, but Mrs. Gibbens refused to consider this and returned for another séance the following week. This time, she convinced James' sister-in-law to accompany her. After this visit, the two women insisted James visit the medium himself, and he agreed.

When James arrived at the Piper home, he was surprised to find the complete absence of Spiritualist props—no cabinet, no red lights, circles of chairs, trumpets or bells. The sitters, of which there were two or three others present, merely sat wherever they liked in the Piper's living room. In addition, Leonora herself was not what James had expected. She was quiet and shy—there was nothing flamboyant about her. She politely warned her guests that there would be nothing sensational about the seance—they should not expect any dishes or plates to fly about. She would simply go into a trance and one of her spirit controls would then take over. There might or might not be messages given—she had no control over that.

James was impressed with what he saw. Leonora was able to summon up the names of his wife's father and even that of a child that he and his wife had lost the previous year. He gave Piper no information to work with and in fact, was purposely quiet throughout the séance.

He later wrote, "My impression after this first visit was that Mrs. Piper was either possessed of supernormal powers or knew the members of my wife's family by sight and had by some lucky coincidence become acquainted with such a multitude of their domestic circumstances as to produce the startling impression which she did. My later knowledge of her sittings and personal acquaintance with her has led me to absolutely reject the latter explanation, and to believe that she has supernormal powers."

James was stumped and made appointments for 25 of his friends to visit her, thus starting research that would continue for the remainder of Leonora's career. Piper's talent was considered to be so extraordinary that she was taken to England for 83 sittings with men considered to be the premiere psychical researchers of the day, including Henry Sidgwick, Sir Oliver Lodge, Sir William Barrett, F.W.H. Meyers and Dr. Walter Leaf. Although she was in a place she'd never been before, was closely watched, and even consented to having her mail opened, Piper did extremely well and continued to amaze even the most hardened investigators.

Nevertheless, it seems to me that even though fraud might have been impossible, she could have been accessing the psychic reservoir or employing superpsi. Some of what we will take a look at in the next chapter, however, cannot possibly be explained by such psychic powers. Continuation of consciousness after death is the only logical explanation.

Chapter Six
More than Fifty Years of Irrefutable Research

Suppose you were changing your son's diaper—let's say he was just beginning to talk and was quite verbally adept at the age of 18 months—and he looked you in the eye and said, "When I was your age, I used to change your diaper."

What would you think?

If your father happened to be deceased, would you possibly think your son might be your father reincarnated? That would make him his own grandfather.

Can something like that happen?

I spoke with someone on my radio show in March 2009 who seems to think so. His name is Jim B. Tucker and he is not a wild-eyed Looney Tune. He's a Phi Beta Kappa graduate of the University of North Carolina, a medical doctor, and a board certified child psychiatrist who serves as medical director of the Child & Family Psychiatry Clinic at the University of Virginia School of Medicine. Dr. Tucker has been studying this possibility in a serious and scientific way.

The University of Virginia Medical School—in what was written about in Chapter One of this book, known as its Division of Perceptual Studies—has been researching the subject of children's memories of past lives since 1961. Much of this work was done by, or under direction of, the late Ian Stevenson, M.D. (1918-2007), who wrote a shelf full of books on the subject, having compiled more than 2500 such cases. At the time I spoke with Dr. Tucker, about 1600 of these had been entered into a computer database along with the information collected on each. This was sorted into about 200 different variables, allowing researchers to comb through and cross tabulate the data to spot trends as well as to categorize and compare the similarities and differences based on various factors and characteristics.

Dr. Stevenson was a methodical and meticulous researcher who graduated first in his medical school class at Canada's McGill University. He never actually claimed reincarnation as fact, but rather, said his cases were "suggestive" of reincarnation. His often-cited first book on the subject was published in 1966 and entitled, *Twenty Cases Suggestive of Reincarnation*.

The cases he studied come from all over the world. When Dr. Stevenson began this research, they were easiest to find in places where people have a belief in reincarnation such as India and Thailand. This may be because parents were not as likely to think a child was imagining a past life, and because they are not likely to be embarrassed to talk about it. Nowadays, however, people in the United States are not as reticent as they once were. Dr. Tucker says that since the University of Virginia set up a web site on this subject ten years ago, he and his colleagues hear from parents "all the time" about their children's memories of past lives.

Nevertheless, in the United States reincarnation is thought by many to go against Christian doctrine, even though recent surveys show that more than twenty percent of Christians believe in reincarnation. The percentage is higher, by the way, among younger adults.

Reincarnation and Christianity

I'd like devout Christians who may be reading this to know about a man I interviewed on my radio show in the spring of 2008. His name is James A. Reid Sr., and he's a Southern Baptist minister, now retired. He holds a Doctor of Ministry degree from San Francisco Theological Seminary. For 15 years he was Chaplain to the Los Vegas strip, where he heard a lot of talk about Edgar Cayce and past lives, which he always dismissed as fantasy thinking. Finally, he got so fed up he decided to write a book denouncing reincarnation as a Biblically untenable doctrine. But Dr. Reid is an honest and mature individual. Once he dug into Church history and the Scriptures, he was forced to change his view. He ended up writing a book that maintains the Bible supports the doctrine of reincarnation. It is called, *BORN AGAIN AND AGAIN AND AGAIN: A Bible-Based View of Reincarnation.*

Reincarnation Was Accepted for 500 Years

Dr. Reid maintains that for the first five hundred year history of the Church, many accepted reincarnation as fact. It wasn't until 553 A.D. that it was condemned by the Council of Constantinople, and then only by a narrow margin. He gives several examples indicating Jesus and others of his time believed in reincarnation. For example, John the Baptist was supposed by many to be the prophet Elijah reincarnated. Jesus himself said this was so. (See Matthew 11:14.) Once, Jesus asked his followers who people thought he (Jesus) was. They replied that many believed him (Jesus) to be one of the prophets—presumably reincarnated, since the last prophet died about 400 years earlier. Also, consider the story of Jesus restoring the sight of the man who had been born blind, as recounted in John 9:1-12, in which Jesus' disciples ask him if the man's sins caused his blindness, or if the sins of his parents had caused him to be born blind.

Since the man was blind from birth, the only way his own sins could have caused his blindness was for him to have sinned in a former life. Jesus did not tell his followers this wasn't possible. To the contrary, he seems to have assumed it was possible, although he gives another reason for the man's blindness, saying, "Neither this man nor his parents sinned, but this happened so that the work of God might be displayed in his life."

Edgar Cayce, whose psychic readings probably did more than anything to promote the concept of reincarnation in the West, was a devout Presbyterian and Sunday school teacher who read the Bible once through for every year of his life. At first, when reincarnation started showing up in his readings, he was baffled and confused. But he reread the Bible and satisfied himself it wasn't anti-Christian.

There are many references to reincarnation in the Bible but believers overlook or misinterpret them because they have been conditioned to think reincarnation is taboo. Kevin Todeschi, Executive Director of the Association for Research and Enlightenment, said on my radio show in November 2007, that he has counted eleven such references in Matthew's gospel alone.

Rebirth Does Not Conflict with Jesus' Teachings

As a regular churchgoer myself, and a follower of Jesus, it's my personal opinion nothing about reincarnation is incompatible with Jesus' message and what he set out to accomplish. Read the Gospels. What he was trying to tell us isn't at all complicated. He put it succinctly in John 15:17: "This is my command: Love each other."

Jesus' main objective is also pretty clear. It's to bring heaven to earth. He talks about this constantly and uses parables to explain what heaven is. For instance, this verse (Matthew 13:44) indicates how wonderful it would be: "The kingdom of heaven is like a treasure hidden in a field. When a man found it, he hid it again, and then in his joy went and sold all he had and bought that field."

Bringing heaven to earth is one of the main points of the prayer Jesus taught that practically everyone in Christendom knows by heart:

". . . Thy kingdom come, Thy will be done, on earth as it is in heaven . . . "

And how does one bring the kingdom of heaven to earth? By loving God first—rather than things such as money and power—and by loving his neighbor as himself. By treating others as he would like and hope to be treated, as in the parable of the good Samaritan. Imagine if everyone did that. . . .

Wouldn't it bring heaven to earth?

The Child Who Is His Grandfather

In the case mentioned at the beginning of this chapter—the 18-month-old child who said he had changed his father's diaper when he was his father's age—the child's mother was the daughter of a Southern Baptist preacher. As you might imagine, she found what her son said to be highly unusual. I asked Dr. Tucker to describe the case when he came on my show, and he obliged.

The child's grandfather had died eighteen months before the child's birth. His first mention of having been his own grandfather was during that change of diapers, but as time went by he made more comments about how he used to be big, and what he did when he was. His mother in particular became interested and began to ask the boy, whose name was Sam, questions. Sam came up with some very specific statements. For instance, she asked him if he had had any bothers or sisters. He said he had had a sister who was killed. In fact the grandfather's sister had been murdered sixty years before.

The parents felt certain the child could not have known this since they had only recently learned about it themselves.

The child also talked about how, at the end of his previous life, his wife would make milkshakes for him every day, and that she made them in a food processor rather than in a blender. This turned out to be true.

When Sam was four years old, his grandmother—his wife in his previous life—died. Sam's dad traveled to where she lived and took care of the estate. When he returned, he brought some family photos with him.

One night Sam's mother had the pictures spread out on the coffee table. Sam walked over and pointed to pictures of his grandfather and said, "Hey, that's me."

To test him she pulled out a class photo from the time the grandfather was in elementary school. Sam ran his finger across the photo, which had sixteen boys in it, and stopped on the one who had indeed been his grandfather.

"That's me," he said.

The Reason Sam May Have Come Back

The grandfather may have come back as the son of his own son because of the relationship—or lack thereof—the two had had in his previous life. The grandfather had not had an open relation with Sam's dad. He had been a very private person. Sam's dad felt that if his father had really returned as his son, his father may have decided to come back to try to develop a closer bond than had existed in their previous relationship. Dr. Tucker said this may be true. When he visited the family he could see that Sam and his dad were very close.

A Dad Determined to Be Reborn

A successful lawyer friend who wishes to remain anonymous related a similar case to me. I'll call him Frank. If his story is true—and I have no reason to doubt it—it demonstrates the tenacity a soul can have if it wishes to incarnate and be close to a specific person.

Frank was divorced. He had two children from the marriage and no intention of having any more—even if he should remarry. One night he had a dream, a very vivid dream such as the one Julie Beischel had when her mother came to her. In his case, Frank's dream was about his father—with whom he had been very close. But his father didn't actually visit him face to face. He called Frank on the phone.

The dream seemed very real and was crystal clear. It took place at Frank's office. As he was talking to his dad, Frank recalled his secretary telling someone who wanted to see him not to interrupt.

"Frank's talking with his father."

"Isn't his father dead?"

"Yes," the secretary said. "But you know Frank. He probably really is talking to his father. You can't go in there."

Frank and his father had quite a conversation—one that

went on for some time. They had a lot to catch up about because Frank's father had been dead for a number of years.

At one point in the conversation, as it was coming to an end, Frank said, "I'm glad you called, Dad. I miss you."

The father replied, "I miss you, too, son. But you know, it may not be as long as you might think before we're together again."

"Uh-oh," Frank said. "Is something going to happen to me?"

"Oh, no, don't worry, son," the father said. "Nothing is going to happen to you."

As you recall, Frank was divorced. But he did have a girlfriend, and you need to know something else in order to fully appreciate this story. Frank had had a disease of the testes that had left him almost sterile—though not completely. He had an extremely low sperm count—about ten percent of normal. His doctor had told him it was highly unlikely he'd ever have more children.

Nevertheless, his girlfriend always took precautions, including the use of a diaphragm and spermicide. But, as you may have guessed, she became pregnant. And you know what? She had a premonition the baby she was carrying was Frank's father—Frank's father's soul—about to reincarnate.

After a good deal of agonizing and debate, she decided to have the pregnancy terminated. Not long afterwards, perhaps because of the disharmony her decision caused, Frank moved on and found another girlfriend.

You guessed it, the next girlfriend also became pregnant—despite what would normally have been ample precautions.

The second girlfriend had her pregnancy terminated.

Keep in mind that Frank was virtually sterile, and they always used birth control because—miraculously, it seemed—the same woman became pregnant a second time. When this happened Frank concluded nothing was going to stop the soul on the other side—the soul who wanted to come through and have him as father. He begged the young woman to go through with the pregnancy.

But she refused and the fetus was aborted, thus ending their relationship.

Shortly afterwards, Frank had another dream—a very vivid dream. He dreamt that he went up to the attic of his house and discovered three little girls there.

Parenthetically, let me say the majority of those who have studied reincarnation, those I've spoken with, believe souls are androgynous—they have no sex—and can incarnate either as males or females.

In his dream about the attic, Frank encountered not boys, but three little girls. One was several years old—the age the baby born of the first pregnancy would have been had she come to term. The second was the age the child of the next pregnancy, and the third was a tiny infant—the age of the third.

In Frank's dream he became enraged and upset upon finding these children in his attic. He lost his temper, found a baseball bat and beat them with it.

Afterwards, still dreaming, Frank's anger dissipated and a sense of terrible remorse came over him. As he sobbed uncontrollably, one of the little girls attempted to console him. Touching his arm, she said, "Don't worry, you didn't hurt us. You can't hurt us. We're already dead."

A Little Girl Recognizes Frank

A few years later, Frank met a woman through his work who had a daughter about one year of age. The little girl's father had died suddenly and unexpectedly before she was born.

Frank thought the woman was attractive and accepted her invitation to come to dinner at her house.

When Frank arrived, the woman was all smiles.

"You look happy," he said as she stepped aside to let him into her house.

"I am," she said. "My daughter just said her first word."

"What was it?" Frank said.

"She said, 'Mamma.'"

Frank entered the house and saw the little girl.

He crouched down to talk to her.

The little girl looked up at him—into his eyes—and with feeling said, "Dadda!"

You guessed it. Frank and the woman were married.

Later, when the little girl was about two years old, she said to her mom one night when the mom was putting her to bed,

"You know, Mom, I'm having trouble remembering."

"What are you having trouble remembering, dear?"

"I remember before, when I was big. And I remember Daddy then. But I don't remember you then—before, when I was big."

Later on, the little girl said a number of other, similar things Frank thinks indicate she was his father reincarnated. She also apparently displayed a number of his father's traits, including peculiar food preferences.

At this writing she is a senior in high school. She and Frank still have a close relationship, but she no longer recalls the time before—when she was big.

A Murder Victim Comes Back

Returning now to the files of the University of Virginia, another interesting case Dr. Tucker related on my show has to do with and Indian girl named Kum Kum, who said she had been murdered in her previous life—poisoned—by her daughter-in-law. Kum Kum said she was from a city of about 200,000 located about 25 miles away. One of the things that makes this a good case is that her aunt wrote down a number of statements—eighteen in all—she made before an effort was undertaken to see if they checked out.

All of them did.

The statements included the name of a son, the name of a grandson, the fact that the son had worked with a hammer.

And a number of other specifics—for example, that she had a sword hanging near the cot where she slept, and a pet snake she fed milk to.

Research led to the woman Kum Kum claimed to have been, who had died five years before she was born. A big family flap had taken place over a will and who would inherit the worldly possessions of the deceased woman's son. Kum Kum had probably been right. Circumstantial evidence indicated the son's wife had poisoned her mother-in-law—the woman Kum Kum insisted she'd been.

What Many Cases Have in Common

These case histories are fascinating and convincing, and we could go on almost indefinitely considering them, individually. After all, there are more than 2500 in UVA's files that have checked out. Instead, let's step back and look at the overall findings of this exhaustive study.

Children who report past-life memories typically begin talking about a previous life when they are two to three years old. You may recall that Dr. Braude said emotional involvement with past-life family members would indicate reincarnation rather than superpsi or the psychic reservoir at work. Well, the children tend to show strong emotional involvement with such memories and often tearfully ask to be taken to the previous family. Once there, not only is a deceased individual usually identified whose life matched the details given, during the visits, children often recognize family members or friends from that individual's life. Tearful reunions are common.

Birthmarks and Birth Defects Provide Evidence

Many children studied also had birthmarks that matched wounds on the body of the deceased individual. To give one example, a boy in Thailand, who said he'd been a schoolteacher in this previous life, was shot and killed when riding his bicycle to school one day. He gave specific details including his name in that life and where he had lived. He continued to make this claim until his grandmother took him to the previous address. The child was able to identify the various members of his previous family by name.

Even more startling, however, he was born with two birth marks: a small round birthmark on the back of his head and a larger, more irregularly shaped one near the front. The woman he claimed was his wife in that life recalled investigators saying her husband had been shot from behind. The investigators said they knew this because he had a typical, small, round entrance wound in the back of his head and a larger, irregular exit wound in front.

In another case, a boy remembered a life in a village not far away in which he had lost the fingers of his right hand in a fodder-chopping machine. The child was born with an intact left hand but the fingers of his right hand were missing.

The average length of time between the death and rebirth of the children in these birthmark cases is only fifteen to sixteen months. As we will see, this sort of thing may happen when the soul takes a shortcut between lives, skipping a process by which the life just lived would have been fully integrated into the soul.

A Fifth of UVA Cases Have Birth Defects

According to Dr. Tucker's book, *Life Before Life* (St. Martin's Griffin, 2005), about 22 percent of the cases in the University's database include birth defects due to wounds suffered in violent deaths in the previous life. Most of the cases come from the Hindu and Buddhist countries of South Asia, the Shiite peoples of Lebanon and Turkey, the tribes of West Africa, and the tribes of northwestern North America.

In 1997 Stevenson published details of 225 cases in a massive work Reincarnation and Biology: A Contribution to the Etiology of Birthmarks and Birth Defects. The same year he presented a summary of 112 cases in a much shorter book, Where Reincarnation and Biology Intersect.

In many cases postmortem reports, hospital records, or other documents were located and consulted that confirmed the location of the wounds on the deceased person in question matched the birthmarks. These often correspond to bullet wounds or stab wounds, and as in the case described above. Sometimes two marks correspond to the points where a bullet entered and then exited the body.

Birthmarks also related to a variety of other wounds or marks, not necessarily connected with the previous personality's death, including surgical incisions and blood left on the body when it was cremated. A woman run over by a train that sliced her right leg in two was reborn with her right leg absent from just below the knee. A man born with a severely malformed ear had been resting in a field at twilight, mistaken for a rabbit, and shot in the ear.

Behavior Traits Also Provide Evidence

Further evidence for reincarnation comes from what might be called behavioral memories. For example, cases exist where children of lower caste Indian families believe they had been upper class Brahmins, and in their view still were. These children would refuse to eat their family's food, which they considered polluted. Conversely, a child remembering the life of a street-sweeper—a very low caste—showed an alarming lack of concern about cleanliness. Some children demonstrate skills they have not learned in their present life, but which the previous personality was known to have had. A number of Burmese children who recalled being Japanese soldiers killed there during World War Two preferred Japanese food such as raw or semi-raw fish over the spicy Burmese fair served by their families.

Many children express memories of the previous life in the games they play. A girl who remembered a previous life as a schoolteacher would assemble her playmates as pupils and instruct them with an imaginary blackboard. A child who remembered the life of a garage mechanic would spend hours under a family sofa "repairing" the car he pretended it to be. One child who remembered a life in which he had committed suicide by hanging himself had the habit of walking around with a piece of rope tied round his neck.

Phobias May Originate in a Former Life

Phobias occur in about a third of the cases and are nearly always related to the mode of death in the previous life. For example, death by drowning may lead to fear of being immersed in water; death from snakebite may lead to a phobia of snakes; a child who remembers a life that ended when he was shot may display a phobia of guns and loud noises. A person who died in a traffic accident may have a phobia of cars, buses, or trucks.

Sexual orientation may also be affected by a previous life. In one of his books, Ian Stevenson wrote, "Such children almost invariably show traits of the sex of the claimed in the previous life. They cross-dress, play the games of the opposite sex, and may otherwise show attitudes characteristic of that sex. As with the phobias, the attachment to the sex and habits of the previous life usually becomes attenuated as the child grows older; but a few of these children remain intransigently fixed to the sex of the previous life, and one has become homosexual."

Certain preferences and cravings can also carry over. They frequently take the form of a desire or demand for particular foods not eaten in the child's present family, or for clothes different from those ordinarily worn by the family members. Other examples include cravings for addictive substances, such as tobacco, alcohol, and other drugs that the previous personality was known to have used.

UVA's Cases May Not Be Representative of the Whole

Dr. Tucker pointed out that the cases he and others have studied may not be typical because most children do not remember past lives. As mentioned, the average time between lives in these cases is only fifteen months or so—although there are outliers that range up to fifty years. In 70 percent of these cases, the previous personality died by unnatural means. Many died young. This may speed up the reincarnation process. The consciousness may come back quickly due to unfinished business, or because he or she feels shortchanged. The quick return may also be the reason past life memories are intact, as well as sexual preferences, cravings and so forth. My guess is that a much longer duration between lives is the norm.

Teachings of the Rosicrucians, a mystical order of which I have been a member and attained the rank of "Adept," say the human personality span is normally about 140 years. If we live 70 years, for example, we can expect to spend 70 years in the realm between lives before we incarnate again. If we live 60 years, we can expect to spend 80 years between lives. The teachings stress, however, that this is a rule of thumb. Centuries could elapse between incarnations, or as with many in the UVA study, the return could come in a matter of months.

Adults Can Also Have Past Life Memories

Memories of past lives also sometimes occur in adults, and such memories can be of lives that took place long ago. I once recalled a romantic interlude from a life as a Russian army officer during the Napoleonic Wars. It happened when I met the same woman in this life. A guest on my show recalled having a spontaneous recollection of a life as a woman that took place in twelfth or thirteenth century France. He was being burned at the stake. He said this was so vivid it seemed more than a memory. He actually felt he was there, subjectively experiencing the ordeal.

He'd been meditating when suddenly it seemed he was back in the skin he'd occupied then—the action taking place around him. Information about who he was and what was taking place was present in his mind as though he had literally been transported back in time and reentered that body. He said that, surprisingly, he did not feel much pain at being burned—his consciousness exited his body as soon as the flames engulfed it. He floated nearby observing his body burn—not feeling any pain at all. Nevertheless, it was a gut wrenching, emotional experience that left him so distraught he secluded himself after reliving the experience and was unable to communicate with others for two or three days.

He said his need to withdraw had not been because of the pain he'd endured. It was a result of the distress he felt over the pain and suffering humanity puts itself through—man's inhumanity to man. He'd been burned at the stake in that life because he'd been a priestess of the Cathar religion, a Gnostic Christian sect persecuted and eventually extinguished by the Roman Catholic Church. His death by fire was just one of many that took place during the twelfth through fourteenth centuries.

Why were these people killed? No doubt they were seen as a threat to those in power, which at that time included leaders of the Church. The Church taught and teaches that salvation comes through belief in Christ and his sacrifice on the cross. Gnostics followed Christ's teachings but believed salvation comes through direct knowledge of God—a direct and personal relationship. Today, many if not all churches foster this direct relationship—a daily walk with God is considered a requisite by most. Catholicism in the time of the Cathars, however, taught that only the clergy could have this direct relationship.

Memory of an Execution at Auschwitz

The same man recalled another past life triggered by a train trip he took in Poland. As the train moved out of the station in Warsaw, memories came crashing down upon him of a lifetime that had ended directly prior to this one. He'd been a Polish Jew—a boy in World War Two.

He was seven years old and an orphan when the Nazis invaded Poland and was swept up and placed in the Warsaw ghetto. He managed to survive as a street urchin for about four years. Then he was rounded up and driven along with other Jews into one of many boxcars of a train headed to Auschwitz.

He recalls vividly what happened next. When the prisoners exited the boxcars, the strong and healthy were herded off in one direction—to perform forced labor, he now assumes. The old and the young—into which category he fell—were taken immediately in a different direction to the "delousing center." There, they were told to remove their clothes and enter a room. About 200 to 250 crowded into a space and packed together like Tokyo commuters on a train. The room, of course, turned out to be a gas chamber, and it wasn't long before lethal gas emerged from the showerheads.

A Quick Exit of the Body to Help Others

Unlike many of those around him, when the poison began to take hold he left his body almost immediately and without much pain. He recalls vividly that many in the chamber were not willing or were unable to accept their deaths, continuing to believe they were there being deloused even after their bodies had died. In addition, there were hundreds, perhaps even thousands of disembodied spirits stuck there from prior mass executions. Instinctively, he seemed to understand their

Life After Death

predicament and held back from entering the tunnel of light. Rather, he stayed behind and was able to help many move along.

Before he left, he was able to help several hundred move to the light. Once enough of the group had caught on to the fact they were dead and needed to move on, the word seemed to spread to others. He was able to both lead and push a sort of daisy chain of souls into and through the tunnel and on to the light.

Getting stuck after death seems to be fairly common, and it's something we all should be concerned about. In many cases, a soul does not realize its body is dead, or can't believe it, and remains in denial. We may be better off to see death coming.

This will be discussed in an upcoming chapter.

Chapter Seven
Life Between Lives

As stated in the previous chapter, cases of reincarnation studied by the University of Virginia may not reflect what normally occurs when someone dies and reincarnates. This may be because most of the UVA cases have to do with souls that reincarnated after a violent death, or a death that came about unexpectedly. The experience of souls in these situations may be very different than that of others who lived a normal length of time, accomplished what they had intended in life, could see the end coming, and were able to prepare for death.

As has been discussed, many who have near death experiences, for example, report passing through what seems a corridor, or a tunnel and into the light where they are often greeted by archetypes or religious figures, and loved ones who have gone before. Some undergo a life review and counseling by entities they believe to be ascended masters and guides. This is not so in most of the cases studied by UVA. In one I read about many years ago, I believe it was in Dr. Stevenson's first book, the reincarnated entity had been attacked in his home by thieves, bound hand and foot with wire, and left to die. He floated out of his body and drifted around the neighborhood until he stumbled upon an opportunity to be reborn. He entered a fetus in his future mother's womb and never encountered a tunnel or saw a light. In his new life, he had birthmarks on his wrists and ankles where his hands and feet had been bound.

It seems possible that in many of the UVA cases some sort of normal progression between lives was skipped. Perhaps some souls who die a normal death and pass through the tunnel and into the light do not reincarnate at all. Maybe others do, but only after a number of steps have been taken, or stages have been passed through. This progression could be what causes memories to be absorbed or incorporated into a person's soul so that, once reborn, past life memories are no longer easily accessed. One may have to know one has died and fully process the former life in order to move past it and start fresh in a new one.

The Five Psychological Stages Preceding Death

In her book, *On Death & Dying* (Simon & Schuster/Collier Books, 1970), Elizabeth Kübler-Ross, M.D. (1926-2004), wrote that terminally ill patients typically pass through five stages as they approach their demise: Denial, anger, bargaining, depression, and finally, acceptance. It should not be surprising, then, that many who die unexpectedly remain in the denial stage even after death. This is supported by findings of The Monroe Institute, the organization mentioned in an earlier chapter that was hired by the United States Government to train remote viewers.

TMI uses a protocol for inducing out-of-body experiences that visitors to weekend retreats and seminars offered by the Institute can try for themselves. Some are successful at achieving out-of-body travel and others are not. Some individuals become very adept at this.

How the Phenomenon of Stuck Souls Was Discovered

In a journey out of the body twenty or so years ago, one of these adepts came across the soul of an English sailor who, in the late 1840s, had died in a shipwreck at sea. The case is similar to the one recounted earlier of a man who had been bricked up behind a wall in the basement of a chateaux in Lorraine. Both men had died and didn't know it with the result they continued pursuing the activity they had been engaged in at the moment of death. In the case of the ghost of Henri's chateaux, this involved screaming for help from behind the brick wall that trapped him. In the case of the British sailor, it involved clinging to a piece of debris from the wreckage of his ship somewhere in the Irish sea—a ship that had gone down in a raging storm after putting out from Liverpool.

The adept from The Monroe Institute who came upon this soul was part of what was called the Explorer Program. In Explorer sessions, the adept places him or herself inside a specially designed sensory depravation chamber. The out-of-body experience (OBE) is initiated through the sound technology developed by Robert Monroe. The explorer wears ear phones, as was the case related earlier about Skip Atwater. A conversation takes place. Communication back and forth between the monitor and the OBE traveler is monitored and recorded.

In the case of the sailor in the Irish sea, the monitor could hear the conversation between the OBE explorer and the sailor—the adept's words to the sailor, and the sailor's responses relayed by the adept.

Time is not experienced in the sub atomic realm of spirit where this was taking place. We will cover why this is so when we review the theories of Thomas Troward in an upcoming chapter. The sailor did not know he'd been clinging to the ship's debris for more than 140 years. His mind created the situation he believed himself to be experiencing. For him, the shipwreck had happened a few hours earlier. The OBE explorer, of course, knew otherwise. She was fully aware more than 140 years must have passed, and his spirit must be stuck. With advice from the monitor listening in, the OBE researcher convinced the shipwrecked sailor of his true situation and sent him to the light.

TMI researchers now believe this the sort of thing is common and is the basis of many hauntings. Someone may die in a house, for example, and either not want to leave or not know he or she is dead.

The Lifeline Program Is Developed

After this episode, Robert Monroe did quite a bit of out-of-body exploring on his own to find out more about this phenomenon. He wrote about his explorations in his book, The Ultimate Journey (Main Street Books, 1996).

An unexpected or violent death is not the only reason souls get stuck. Some are caught up in materialistic ideas and pursuits and have no idea anything spiritual exists. This may happen to the pseudo skeptics who maintain doggedly, even in the face of scientific evidence to the contrary, that nothing exists that is not available to the five physical senses. They may never think to look for the tunnel and the light. Others, who see the tunnel and the light, may avoid going to it out of fear of what they may encounter—judgment for their transgressions.

A Psychiatrist Helps Stuck Souls See the Light

A while back I interviewed Shakuntala Modi, M.D., a psychiatrist who specializes in ridding people of earthbound spirits who attach themselves to the living and cause all manner of problems, both physical and mental. Her book is called *Remarkable Healings: A Psychiatrist Discovers Unsuspected Roots of Mental and Physical Illness* (Hampton Roads, 1998). Essentially, she speaks with these spirits through her hypnotized patients and attempts to convince them, usually with success, they should look up, see the light, and go to it. She tells them they will find comfort there and that no one other than themselves will judge them.

Spirit Possession Does Happen

Some readers will find it difficult to believe spirit possession is real, even though references to it in literature go back thousands of years. Think about it. If some spirits remain on the earth plane after death, why should it be unusual for them to attach themselves to the living?

A soul entering a fetus may even be a form of possession. Of course, this must happen at conception. Otherwise, how would a fetus develop without a hand or leg, or other missing body part, as happened to many in the UVA study? If the soul had entered at a later time, the fetus would already have begun developing the missing body part.

Who is likely to suffer from obsession or possession? A child whose personal boundaries are weak, or even an adult, who has been weakened because of illness or an accident, may be vulnerable. Most are invaded by wandering spirits, or even relatives, who have died. Dr. Modi says possession by evil spirits, demons, or an entity identifying himself as Satan is rare but not unheard of.

A number of mental health professionals, including psychiatrists and psychologists, now treat possession, or its lesser form, obsession. Officials of the Roman Catholic Church still train a number of priests each year to conduct exorcisms, and they officially designate and specify those deemed qualified for the task. Yet, the Church has strictly controlled exorcism in modern times. According to one source, a 27 page ritual exists that is followed to drive out demons. Moreover, an exorcism isn't something a parish priest can decide on his own to do. Church canon requires an exorcism be performed only upon a direct order "of the bishop, after two careful investigations, based on positive indications that possession is in fact present."

The Catholic Church Still Performs Exorcisms

According to the memoirs of Cardinal Jacques Martin [no relation], the former prefect of the pontifical household, Pope John Paul II successfully exorcised a woman in 1982. She was brought to him writhing on the ground. Father Gabriele Amorth told *La Stampa,* an Italian newspaper, that Pope John Paul II successfully conducted three exorcisms during his pontificate. Amorth said, "He carried out these exorcisms because he wanted to give a powerful example. He wanted to give the message that we must once again start exorcising those who are possessed by demons . . . I have seen many strange things [during exorcisms] . . . objects such as nails spat out. The devil told a woman that he would make her spit out a transistor radio and lo and behold she started spitting out bits and pieces of a transistor radio. I have seen levitations, and a force that needed six or eight men to hold the person still. Such things are rare, but they happen."

Reader's Digest Press published an absolutely fascinating book on this subject in 1976 called *Hostage to the Devil.* It was written by Malachi Martin (1921 – 1999), also no relation, a former Jesuit Professor at the Pontifical Biblical Institute in Rome, who studied at Oxford and has a doctorate in Semitic languages, archeology, and Oriental history. The book gives extensive background about and relates the full details of five actual exorcisms conducted under the sanction of the Roman Catholic Church. Do not read this book at night if you are alone. Apparently, the depiction of an exorcism related in the popular book and movie, The Exorcist, is accurate because that's what the exorcisms Malachi Martin described were like. It's a gross understatement to say that Satan and his buddies are a really, really nasty bunch. You thought Jeffery Dahlmer was sick? He was a Boy Scout by comparison.

Non-Religious Exorcisms

In recent years, a number of psychiatrists, psychologists, and other mental health practitioners have gotten into the business of what they call "depossession." They'd rather call it depossession than exorcism I suppose because they don't approach it from a religious perspective. They say they rarely encounter Satan and his demons although they tend to agree Satan and his minions exist, and that obsession or possession by them can happen. According Dr. Louise Ireland-Frey, a psychiatrist, "[Satan and demons] do not belong to the human kingdom, being the negative aspect, composed of the 'fallen angels' and their slaves. This is not drawn from a religious source . . . I have been told these things by the dark entities [I have] encountered. A number of them have told us that they are delighted to get us to believe that they exist only when we think of them, speak of them, and 'believe in' them—it makes their work of invading easier! On the other hand, thinking fearfully of them, brooding compulsively, talking often of them certainly does predispose a person to attracting their focused attention."

The approach used to depossess a patient who is afflicted in this way is less confrontational than that of an exorcism by a Catholic priest. In addition, the therapist routinely tries to help the invading spirit find its way into the light.

Let me pause here to say, much has already been written about this. I conducted a Google search and turned up a web site that offered a dozen different books on the subject. I'm going to relate some of what Dr. Louise Ireland-Frey (1912-1914) has to say in her book, *Freeing the Captives: The Emerging Therapy of Spirit Attachment* (Hampton Roads, 1999) because her credentials are strong. She was a Phi Beta Kappa graduate of Colorado University, had a Master of Arts degree from Mount Holyoke College in Massachusetts, and a medical degree from Tulane University.

Dr. Louise Ireland-Frey spent a full career as a medical doctor and psychiatrist before, at the age of 67, she began using hypnotism to help those who suffer past-life trauma. She also uses it to detach earthbound spirits who may be causing trouble for her patients. She says that when her clients are regressed to a previous life and come to the death experience terminating that lifetime, it's possible to continue the regression past the physical death and on into the after-death state. Similarly, when she contacts earthbound entities—those who may or may not have attached themselves to a living person—she can also ask them to recall the circumstances of their physical death. Dr. Ireland-Frey uses an intermediary to make this contact. Essentially, she hypnotizes someone, either the patient she is trying to help, or a willing assistant, and has the hypnotized individual "channel" the earth-bound entity.

Using this procedure she has learned what we already surmised from NDEs. A person's consciousness typically floats above the body for a short time after death. The disembodied consciousness usually feels free and light and relieved, and it senses it can go wherever it seems to be drawn. At this point it might be drawn through what seems a tunnel and into the light. This light is perceived as alive and sentient, a Being of Light who welcomes the personality with understanding, kindness, and love. She says that in fact most people find themselves going to a state that is peaceful and beautiful. Only an occasional person reports a chilly, lonely, or horrifying, hell-like experience.

She has also learned through this procedure the stages after death that we've already touched on—the life review, for example, in which the activities, actions, thoughts, and words of the entire life are reviewed and evaluated as to their value and impact on others. The individual sees both his or her successes, weaknesses, and failures, and in this way judges for him or herself the worth and value of the life just past. Another stage is one Ireland-Frey calls the "cleansing," which is often described as the feeling of being embraced or surrounded by light.

It seems to me the world would be a much better place if everyone accepted this model of what happens. So many of us now believe that when they die, that's it—nothingness—and they live their lives accordingly. They think, "Might as well live it up—who cares who gets hurt in the process?"

If so, they may be sorry they didn't read this book. Experience for the sake of experience becomes their life goal, rather than achievement, service to others, and the development of character.

Young people take heed. And don't be discouraged while reading this if you are getting on in years. It's never too late to make amends—even to those who may have gone before you. Think about them. Picture them in your mind's eye, and tell them you're sorry. It certainly can't hurt, and will probably help a great deal.

And it's never too late to be learning things you can carry over to the next life. Find something you feel passionate about and pursue it. When you come back next time, you will have a head start on what may be your life's calling. Want to be a novelist? Start writing that novel. It doesn't matter if it doesn't get published this time around. You're learning to write. Knowledge is one of the few things you can take with you, remember?

How Souls Become Invaders of the Living

As we have already learned, not all souls go through the stages outlined above. As was touched on, a person who is heavy with negative emotions and undesirable habits such as rage, cruelty, greed and so forth may be too negative to be attracted to the light, and will turn away, perhaps not even perceiving it, and go to a "place"—a vibrational frequency, or "dimension"—that is appropriate to its present nature, i.e., dark and heavy. Ireland-Frey says souls are a little like substances suspended in water, the "heaviest" after death sink to the lowest astral levels, the "lightest" float to the upper levels, and the rest find the appropriate levels in-between.

Many die not having a clear idea of what to expect after death and find themselves bewildered upon discovering they are still aware. It is as though they are alive, but their bodies are dead and they can't reenter them. Rather than going to the light or finding an appropriate vibrational level, they remain on the earth plane where they are able to see and hear living persons but are invisible and inaudible to them. These souls are likely to find this situation frustrating. Not knowing what to do or where to go, many such disembodied spirits start to wander, either aimlessly, or perhaps to some chosen place or to be near a special person.

Some wanderers remain in the area of their body—which may now be buried. I have a friend, for example, who says he is sensitive to the presence of the disembodied and will not go near a graveyard. Others may find a home in a house or other building and become the "ghosts" who haunt these places.

According to Dr. Ireland-Frey, many wanderers find a place that seems lighter or warmer than the chilly darkness of the earth-bound state in which they have been, and it turns out to be the body or aura of a living person—often without either the living host or the invading spirit being aware of the relationship.

What sort of person is a likely host for an invading spirit? As briefly noted, a person whose aura is weak or "open" is most susceptible. This may be because the individual has been in an accident, or suffered an illness, been under an anesthetic for an operation, or recently suffered an emotional shock such as grief or fear. Children, whose auras are not yet fully protective, are also vulnerable. In addition, Occult activities such working a Ouija board may open an invasion path.

Five Degrees of Spirit Attachment

Dr. Ireland-Frey has, as have other therapists, identified several degrees of closeness of such attachments. The first level is that of temptation of the living person by an aspect of the wanderer. This is not really an overwhelming compulsion but the thought or idea of doing or saying something that is contrary to the basic personality of the living individual—something out of character.

The second level is called "influencing" or "shadowing." In this instance, the disembodied entity is affecting the host person mildly or intermittently, as with mood swings, irrational moments, sudden inexplicable fears or depressions.

Third, in situations where the entity is affecting the host's personal feelings and habits more noticeably and frequently, the word "oppression" or "harassing" is used. Dr. Ireland-Frey says someone who is clairvoyant may be able to see the entity attached to the host's aura or within it.

Obsession is the fourth step up. Here Dr. Ireland-Frey's definition differs slightly from that of the Roman Catholic Church. She says it's a remarkably common condition in which the entity may invade not only the psyche but also the physical body of the host and meld its own personality traits and former bodily feelings with those of the host, often to the confusion and bewilderment of that person. The affected person may become aware of persistent pains, sudden changes in emotions unlike his or her normal feelings, unfamiliar attitudes, or even unnatural traits and talents.

And finally, number five is "possession," the condition wherein the invading entity takes over the body of the host completely, pushing out the host's soul and expressing its own words, feelings, and behaviors through the host's body. Dr. Ireland-Frey says complete possession is rare, and can be spectacular when it happens. Sometimes it may alternate with obsession. A case when a person suddenly goes berserk, for example, may be the result of sudden, complete possession. She writes that she has personally seen only one case of complete possession.

Support for Dr. Ireland-Frey

Dr. Ireland-Frey's observations dovetail in many respects with the findings of Robert Monroe, founder of The Monroe Institute. In addition to souls stuck on earth, Monroe found there to be bands of energy around the planet where people are stuck. In at least one of these, he found souls caught up in hedonistic pursuits where they were mindlessly pursuing orgiastic sexual activity. He also found that physical sites exist on the planet where people are caught up as well. As a result, he devoted a good deal of his time and energy to helping people move from these sites to what he called "The Reception Center"—the realm of light at the end of the tunnel. While in the out-of-body state, Monroe was able to see these discarnates, and they were able to see him. He was able to explain to them that they were stuck and was able to coax them along.

The Lifeline Program

As previously mentioned, Monroe and his staff at The Monroe Institute developed a protocol for helping lost or stuck souls find their way and, as I understand it, this is still put to use today following major disasters that suddenly take the lives of many people. Groups of graduates of the Monroe Institute teamed up after the Oklahoma City bombings, and again after the 911, attacks to help free stuck souls, following those disasters. A total of 168 persons were killed in Oklahoma City. Apparently more than half were stuck. It's not surprising many did not know they had died since the bombing came without warning. The attack on the Twin Towers caused many more deaths, but only a small percentage became stuck. Most were not killed instantly. They knew they were going to die. Although they went through a horrifying experience, most passed into the light soon after death. To me, this is preferable to becoming stuck in place and time.

It must have been a big job freeing so many stuck souls, but the out-of-body rescuers were able to confront them, explain the situation and lead them to the light. As they approached the reception center—the realm of light—beings of light came forward, took over from the rescuers and helped the newly deceased transition to their new surroundings.

You may be wondering why the beings of light didn't go down to the physical plane to help those stuck. Because of different frequencies in the various realms or levels of the spirit world, most beings that reside in the realm of light and higher are unable to descent to the earth plane. Thus, the out-of-body explorers performed an important service that may otherwise never have taken place.

OBE Explorers Can Go into the Light

While beings of light cannot descend to earth, at least some OBE adepts are able to proceed into the realm of light and actually meet with friends and relatives who have passed on. On occasion, prior students and living friends have visited Robert Monroe himself, who died in 1995.

One might wonder what people do to amuse themselves while they are dead, or between lives, and residing in the realm of light or some higher level of non physical reality. The answer is, "Whatever they want." In that realm, our thoughts instantly create our reality and environment. Robert Monroe, who was perhaps the most accomplished and extensively traveled out-of-body adept said that in the early stages following a normal death, souls may recreate the living environment they have just left. Monroe visited a deceased neighbor of his, a physician in life, and found him working in a garden identical to the one located behind his home in the life just concluded. References to this sort of thing can be found in ancient literature such as the *Tibetan Book of the Dead*.

A soul often processes the life just past by recreating various aspects of it during what might be called a period of assimilation. This is what many of the University of Virginia subjects skipped. Over time—a paradox because there is no time—the personality of the former life becomes incorporated into the soul, after which it may or may not choose to incarnate once again.

I'm willing to bet, however, most souls incarnate many times. Next, we will look at one way many believe soul evolution, through multiple incarnations, may actually work.

Chapter Eight
The Cosmology of Soul Evolution

Concerning human evolution through reincarnation, one school of thought has to do with Michael cosmology. Michael is an arbitrary name given to what some believe to be an entity comprised of about 1050 human souls that exists on a higher plane of consciousness than those of us here in physical reality. Michael is thought to communicate with incarnate earthlings through a dozen or so channels or mediums. These so-called channels have written a number of books. The first was published in 1979, written by Chelsea Quinn Yarbro, called *Messages from Michael on the Nature of the Evolution of the Human Soul*. To get an indication of how widely known the Michael cosmology has become, I plugged the words "Michael Teachings" into Google. A total of 62.5 million hits turned up. I'd say that's pretty widespread.

According to Michael via his channels, the human population on earth is made up of five different soul age categories: Infant, Baby, Young, Mature, and Old. Within each soul age are seven steps or stages, making 35 stages (5 x 7 = 35) in all that are passed through before a soul stops incarnating.

Each step or stage takes one or more lifetimes to complete. I have been told that on average about 110 to 120 lifetimes are required for a soul to pass through all 35. Some souls take many more, some less, but even so, a soul's journey is not finished once it stops incarnating. A number of non physical planes are said to exist that must also be traversed on a soul's journey back to the godhead, or Tao, as Michael refers to God—the ground of being or Universal Mind that gives rise to all that is. Once reunited with the godhead, a soul may decide to go back to square one and begin the long journey—called a "grand cycle"—once again. According to a Michael reading I had done on myself in preparation for an interview with well-known Michael channel Shepherd Hoodwin, I am on my ninth grand cycle, and my soul age this time through is the seventh level of the mature stage (see the chart he prepared for me on the page opposite). If this is true, I calculate I've got about 21 and probably more lifetimes to go before I stop incarnating.

Wears me out to think about it.

The Michael cosmology may or may not be the way things really are, but I have a friend I've known for more than twenty years—a successful and intelligent guy whom I trust—who tells me he's in touch on a regular basis with both Michael and another group soul entity on an even higher plane. He has given the name Group Seven to this even higher plane entity. He says Group Seven confirms the Michael cosmology in principle if not in every specific detail.

A Sixteen-Year-Old's Guides Explain Life

The same friend had an extraordinary experience at the age of 16, which says a lot about our existence as human souls who have incarnated here on earth. This man is now 64 years old and the head of a sizable law firm. As a successful lawyer who knows some of his clients and potential clients will think he belongs in the loony bin after they read this story, he asked me not to use his real name. So I'll call him Thomas—a name he says he once had in a prior life.

Thomas did not have an easy childhood. His mother was a paranoid schizophrenic. He knew this, including the terminology, because his father was a psychiatrist. Who knows . . . maybe the dad married Thomas' mom because he thought he could cure her if he devoted enough time and energy to the project, and really worked at it.

He was wrong.

The result was Thomas never knew how his mother was going to react. His life was in constant turmoil. On top of this, he had fallen in love with his best friend's girlfriend and the girlfriend had given him indications she felt the same toward him. Of course, he did not want to hurt his friend, but at the age of 16 those infamous male hormones were raging and he was upset and confused.

The night the visit with his guides took place, his best friend was spending the night with him, in his bedroom, in a twin bed just a few feet away. It was 3:30 a.m.; his friend was fast asleep. Thomas was wide-awake—wondering what to do, and wishing fervently he'd never been born. Then he wouldn't have all these problems to deal with.

Life After Death

Suddenly, a tornado-like vortex swooped down from above and yanked his consciousness out of his body. It seemed to catapult him up through the roof of his house in a arch like a Fourth of July rocket.

Within seconds Thomas found himself high above the earth looking down. He could see the whole of its curvature. The outline of the east coast was apparent because of the twinkling lights of the cities. He could look out over the Atlantic and see the demarcation of dark and light as dawn approached. Looking up, the firmament of the sky was nothing less than spectacular—thousands or perhaps millions of stars sparkling above.

"While I was on the way up," Thomas told me, "I didn't have time to wonder if this was a dangerous situation I was in. But that thought did cross my mind once the movement stopped."

"But you didn't have a body," I said.

"Exactly—that was my immediate response as well. I didn't know how I'd gotten there, or even what part of me was actually there, but I didn't have a body—so what was there to worry about?"

Thomas said he could see without eyes, was fully present and aware and was wondering how this could be, when he heard a barely audible pop.

"It resembled the slight pop one might hear if one is in a silent room and a bubble travels up through the neck of a long neck beer bottle and out the top. This carried with it the sense it was coming from the top of my head—the head I didn't have.

"When this occurred, the earth disappeared. The sky disappeared. The stars—everything was gone. In the place I associated with my location was a faint glimmer of flickering light, a sort of dotted outline, which I took to be some sort of consciousness or spiritual essence."

Thomas says he thought if this flickering light represented him, then perhaps there were others in this space.

"Then I saw—in what seemed the distance—other flickers of light. Many of them. I wondered if they might also be discarnate beings, so I asked the question, 'Is any body there?'

"As far as I was concerned, I vocalized this, but of course I had no vocal cords because I had no body."

I asked Thomas, "Did any one answer?"

"An answer came immediately. It was, 'Yes.' And these string-like flickering light beings moved toward me and surrounded me. I'm not sure how many there were but I would say about three dozen.

"In the dialog that ensued they all seemed to talk with a single voice—sort of like surround sound, or you might say, quadraphonic."

"Then what happened?" I asked.

"A dialog—I asked them a number of questions and they answered."

"This is fascinating," I said. "Tell me, what did you ask them?"

"My first question was, 'Where am I?'"

"And?"

"Not long after all this happened, I made copious notes and eventually wrote them up, so I can tell you exactly what they said. They said, 'You are in a place that is no place.'

"'What does that mean?' I said, and they said, 'You are outside of space and time as you know it.'

"'What am I doing here?'

"They said, 'We brought you here because we have some very important things to tell you.'

"'Oh, okay,' I said. 'Who are you?'

"'We are your guides.'

"This was in 1960, and I was 16 years old. I knew nothing about such things. I had no idea what they were talking about. So I said, 'What are guides?'

"They said, 'You can think of us as that which is both you and not you.'

"'Me and not me?'"

I couldn't help breaking in and said, "Sounds like, 'What is the sound of one hand clapping?'"

"Exactly," Thomas said. "So then I said that if you're not going to tell me what guides are, can you at least tell me what guides do?

"And they went on to give a beautiful and quite comforting explanation. They said everyone—all living people—have guides. Guides are souls who sign on to facilitate the development of those of us who are embodied."

I said, "Did they give you any advice about your current

situation? About your dilemma concerning your friend and his girlfriend and wishing you had never been born?"

"They did," Thomas said. "After we got through the explanation of who they were, I asked them what important message they had brought me here to tell.

"They said, 'The message is, your life is your own. It belongs to you.'

"I said, 'Who else would it belong to?'

"They said, 'We mean, you are free to do anything you want with your life, or to do nothing with it at all. You can be whatever you want, you can do whatever you want, you can say whatever you want, you can think and feel whatever you want, and whatever you do or don't do with it is perfectly okay.'

"And they went on to say, and this was the heart of the matter, 'Even if you should decide to self destruct'—they didn't use the term, suicide—'even if you should decide to terminate your life because it's unpleasant, or for whatever reason, that's perfectly okay. You may have been taught in school, or in church, that it's not okay, that it's some kind of a sin, that you will go to hell, or whatever—forget all that. It's simply not true. None of that is the way things really are—"

I couldn't help myself, and broke in again, "But there must be some consequences—"

Thomas said, "Oh, they didn't say there wouldn't be consequences. At this point, I started getting on the defensive. I saw where they were going and told them to wait a minute—

I hadn't been planning to self-destruct—or kill myself, or anything like that.

"And they said, 'You had not reached that point yet. But if the thoughts you were having of wishing you did not exist had been followed to their conclusion—if we had not intervened—you would have reached that point. And in some other situations, you may reach that point. And we are here to tell you, that's okay. You won't be judged.

"And then they delivered the punch line. They said, 'But we want you to know that choice would be a waste of time.'"

I said, "Well, how does that work? What happens? Do you have to come back and do it all over again?"

Thomas said, "Exactly—let me tell you. As a 16 year old, when they threw out the words 'waste of time,' that was something I could appreciate. I said, 'Waste of time? What does that mean?'

"They answered by giving me an explanation of the way life and evolution work. In summary, they said we go through a potentially infinite number of lifetimes and for the most part we choose our lifetimes, and what we're likely to experience in each. The thing that had been completely erroneous in my thinking and outlook before they brought me to that place was the idea I could cease to exist.

"'You can terminate a lifetime,' they said, 'but you cannot cease to exist. There is only life. If you decide to exit the one you are in you will simply have to come back and face the same situations again until you deal with and get through them. That's the way it is. Once you have started on a curriculum, you have to see it through."

I said, "That reminds me of the movie, Groundhog Day. The main character gets stuck living the same day over and over again, until he gets it right. Only then does he finally move on."

"A perfect allegory for the human condition," Thomas said.

I asked Thomas why he thought his guides had intervened, that plenty of people commit suicide, and their guides don't stop them.

He told me it was because he had committed suicide in other lives and had a tendency to do so. For this reason, they had been quick to act.

I guess they were tired of him wasting time.

By the way, Thomas was sent back to his body and slept soundly for what was left of the night. And in case you're wondering, he did not pursue his best friend's girlfriend. Two days following his extraordinary meeting with his guides—after he had started a job as a lifeguard for the summer—he met a girl and fell head over heels. His best friend's girlfriend was quickly—and completely—forgotten.

Chapter Nine
The Science of Reincarnation

According to Dr. Tucker, for individual cases he and his colleagues have studied, it is possible to come up with arguments that cast doubt on reincarnation as the cause, but reincarnation is the only viable explanation to explain all the UVA cases when viewed as a whole. Julie Beischel will no doubt go ahead with her research to find out if psychics are using the psychic reservoir, ESP or superpsi to give information about discarnates. What she learns will surely be interesting. But it seems to me the continuation of consciousness of specific individuals has been clearly demonstrated by Ian Stevenson's and Jim Tucker's research. A psychic reservoir, ESP or superpsi, can in no way explain what often accompanies children's memories of past lives—birthmarks that mimic the wounds that ended the past life, the strong emotion many of the children feel about their past life and the loved ones they left behind. It cannot explain food preferences, sexual orientation, phobias, and cravings on the part of some for alcohol or tobacco. If you want to know more about this, I recommend Dr. Tucker's book, *Life Before Life*.

The Mind Separate from the Body

As was covered in some detail in Chapter One, research by UVA's Division of Perceptual Studies clearly indicates that our mind or soul—what Stevenson called the "reincarnating personality"—must be able to exist independently of the brain and body in some sort of mental space or discarnate realm.

The database at the University of Virginia indicates that about one in five children reporting past life memories also report memories of the time spent between the past life and this one. Stevenson theorized there might be an intermediate vehicle, made of "nonmaterial mind stuff" that imprints the embryo or fetus with memories of injuries or other markings of the previous body, together with likes, dislikes, and other attitudes.

Rupert Sheldrake, a British biochemist, graduate of Cambridge University and former Royal Society research fellow, has set forth a hypothesis that explains this. According to Sheldrake, the growth, development and the programmed behavior of organisms are governed by fields which exist much like fields of gravity or electromagnetism, and that these fields change and evolve as a species changes and evolves. Each plant, animal and human has its own field which is part of a larger field of its species just as a radio show has its own particular frequency but is nonetheless part of the full band of radio frequencies on the AM or FM radio dial.

Sheldrake is not the only one to have come up with such a theory. A man named Harold S. Burr, Ph.D., (1889-1973) did also. Dr. Burr was E. K. Hunt Professor Emeritus, Anatomy, at Yale University School of Medicine and a member of the faculty of medicine for more than forty years. From 1916 to the late 1950's, he published, either alone or with others, more than ninety-three scientific papers. Dr. Burr maintained that all living things—from men to mice, from trees to seeds—are molded and controlled by electro-dynamic fields, which he was able to measure and map with standard voltmeters. He maintained that these "fields of life," or L-fields as he called them, are the basic blueprints of all life.

Morphogenetic Fields and Genes Work Together

Sheldrake's theory is essentially the same. According to him, genes and morphogenetic fields work together to create our bodies. Genes account for such things as hair and eye color, and other inherited features. Morphogenetic fields guide the cells of a growing fetus to become a kidney or a foot or a brain while an animal or human embryo is forming in the womb.

Traditional biology assumes genes are programmed with the purpose of each new cell and direct it to form whatever body part it is assigned to, but this has never been demonstrated. Sheldrake says genes dictate the primary structure of proteins, not the individual parts of the body. According to currently accepted theory, given the right genes and hence the right proteins, and the right systems by which protein synthesis is controlled, an organism is supposed to assemble itself. But how does this actually work? As Rupert Sheldrake once wrote, "This is rather like delivering the right materials to a building site at the right times and expecting a house to grow spontaneously."

Physiologists do their best to explain the functioning of plants and animals in mechanistic terms, but explanations of some phenomena are sketchy at best. Sheldrake believes the following can be explained by the existence of morphogenetic fields: Formation of the structure of organisms, instinctive behavior, learning, and memory.

Sheldrake's theory also clears up certain mysteries that currently remain with respect to the theory of evolution. According to the fossil record, a species can remain virtually unchanged for many millennia and then alter dramatically during an epoch when environmental conditions shift. This happens so quickly that scientists often are unable to find evidence of the transition. An eminent authority on evolution, Stephen Jay Gould (1941 – 2002), once wrote, "The extreme rarity of transitional forms in the fossil record persists as the trade secret of paleontology. The evolutionary trees that adorn our textbooks have data only at the tips and nodes of their branches; the rest is inference, however reasonable, not the evidence of fossils."

One Way Evolution Might Work

It seems a reasonable possibility we humans and everything else in the universe evolved out of an organizing intelligence that at this point I shall call spirit. In the beginning, spirit created an almost infinite number of variations of living things. Let's say they were one celled animals in the sea.

Those that were most suited to the environment survived. They reproduced by the millions, each offspring slightly different from its siblings. More complicated forms were the result. Again, those best suited to the environment survived and reproduced. And so on and so on.

As evolution progressed, living organisms themselves developed intelligence. This intelligence impressed itself upon the organizing intelligence of spirit, and the organizing intelligence of spirit went to work to create ever more sophisticated and evolved adaptations. The result of this process can be seen in ever-increasing levels of intelligence displayed by ever more evolved life forms. As intelligence evolves it becomes increasingly self-aware.

Let's say there are now animals walking around on land that are at least somewhat self-aware. One such animal eats leaves and lives in an environment that's changing from forest to savanna. Plenty of leaves were available to eat in the forest. But dryer conditions are developing, punctuated by rainy spells, and much of the low-lying vegetation has died off and been replaced by grass. Some trees are able to survive the dry spells, and more and more, the leaves that remain in this changing environment are found on trees that tend to be fairly high off the ground.

Perhaps this animal walks each day by trees the leaves of which are too high for him to reach. He thinks to himself, "Doggone it, if only I had a longer neck I could feast on those leaves up there." In some way or other this remedy to the predicament forms in the animal's subconscious mind, which is an aspect of the species' morphogenetic field. Newborns of this species begin being born with longer necks as a result, and the animal we know as a giraffe develops in a short period of time. Natural selection also favors those with longer necks and works together with the morphogenetic field in a push-me pull-me effect.

Tasmanian Devils Show Rapid Evolution

A recent example may be that of the Tasmanian devil, reported on in a July 15, 2008, Associated Press article. Researchers at the University of Tasmania in Australia wrote up the case. Faced with an epidemic of cancer that cuts their lives short, Tasmanian devils have begun breeding at much younger ages than one would expect.

"We could be seeing evolution occurring before our eyes. Watch this space!" zoologist Menna Jones of the university was quoted as having said.

Tasmanian devils live on the island of Tasmania, south of Australia. They weigh 20 to 30 pounds and were named devils by early European settlers because the furry black marsupials produce a fierce screech and can be bad-tempered.

Since 1996 a contagious form of cancer called devil facial tumor disease has been infecting these animals and is invariably fatal, causing death between the ages of two and three.

In the past devils would live five to six years, breeding at ages two, three and four, but with the new disease, even females who breed at two may not live long enough to rear their first litter.

Jones, who has been studying the animals' life cycles since before the disease outbreak, noted that there has been a 16-fold increase in breeding at age one. She reported her findings in the July 14, 2008 edition of Proceedings of the National Academy of Sciences.

The disease could cause the devils to become extinct in 25 years or so, she said, but this change to younger breeding may slow population decline and reduce the chance of them disappearing.

The Panda's Thumb

If you've ever been to the National Zoo in Washington, you've probably watched the giant pandas eating bamboo leaves. They take stalk after stalk and slide them between thumb and forefinger, stripping them, then popping this mouthwatering high-fiber food in their mouths. You may have wondered how these big guys got thumbs since primates are the ones with opposing digits. Pandas belong to the family *Procyonidae* (raccoons, kinkajous, et cetera) of the order *Carnivora*, one of the hallmarks of which is that all five digits on the front paw point forward and have claws for ripping flesh.

On close inspection you'll find that the panda's thumb is not a thumb at all but a "complex structure formed by marked enlargement of a (wrist) bone and an extensive rearrangement of musculature." Not having the thumb needed to make bamboo eating easy, the panda took what he had to work with and evolved one of a makeshift variety, according to biologist Stephen Jay Gould, who also wrote, "The panda's thumb provides an elegant zoological counterpart to Darwin's orchids. An engineer's best solution is debarred by history. The panda's true thumb is committed to another role, too specialized for a different function to become an opposable, manipulating digit. So the panda must use parts on hand and settle for an enlarged wrist bone and a somewhat clumsy, but quite workable, solution." Gould added, "Odd arrangements and funny solutions are the proof of evolution—paths that a sensible God would never tread but that a natural process, constrained by history, follows perforce."*

Where Memories Reside

Morphogenetic fields also explain a phenomenon of memory that has neuroscientists puzzled: where it is located in the brain. One way research on this subject has been conducted is to train an animal to do something and then to cut out parts of its brain in an effort to find where the memory was stored. As Sheldrake has written, "But even after large chunks of their brains have been removed—in some experiments over 60 percent—the hapless animals can often remember what they were trained to do before the operation."

Several theories have been put forth to explain this including backup systems and holograms, but the obvious one in light of Sheldrake's hypothesis is that the memory may not be in the brain at all. This has been proven by the past-life research conducted by the University of Virginia in that subjects report memories from between lives when they have no physical body or brain. I asked Dr. Tucker about this. He said brains are needed to recall memories, but it appears brains are not where memories are stored.

The bottom line is, scientists have been looking in the wrong place. To quote Sheldrake again, "A search inside your TV set for traces of the programs you watched last week would be doomed to failure for the same reason: The set tunes in to TV transmissions but does not store them." In other words, the brain is a physical link to the memory located either in our morphogenetic field, or perhaps in our own little cubby in the psychic reservoir.

Instincts May Be Shared Memories

It seems logical to me the morphogenetic fields of individual humans blend into the overall morphogenetic field of humankind. Each one affects the whole in terms of where the species stands in evolution. The same is true of species of animals. This has obvious implications in the explanation of instinctive behavior. The collective field of a species that is hunted—deer, for example—learns over time to be afraid of man. An individual deer does not have to learn this after birth. He is born with it, and we label it "instinctive behavior." It's part of the collective memory of deer that is contained in the morphogenetic field of the species.

Adherents to the "survival of the fittest" theory will argue that of the many deer that are born each spring, those that possess a natural inclination to skittishness are more likely to reach the age of reproduction, and this is what has caused the trait to develop into an instinct over time. This makes sense as well, so it's hard to argue. My guess is—since most things have more than one cause—that both theories are correct and in fact work together as written above in the hypothetical case of the evolution of giraffes.

Other Evidence of Morphogenetic Fields

The fact of a collective morphogenetic field helps explain the behavior of societal insects, fishes and birds. For example, we've all seen swarms of gnats, schools of fish, or flocks of birds behaving as though they were a single organism as they glide through the air or water, turning and diving as though they form one unified whole. Spend some time at an aquarium watching a school of fish. Something is sure to cause a minor explosion in their midst, producing momentary chaos as individuals scatter a short distance from their original positions. But within seconds, they will regroup and become a single moving organism once more.

The behavior of some species is truly amazing, or would be without Sheldrake's and Dr. Burr's theory. Key West silver-sided fish, for example, will organize themselves around a barracuda in a shape that seems dictated by risk. The distance between the school and the barracuda is widest at the predator's mouth and narrowest at the tail, where the threat of being eaten is the least.

In the world of insects, African termites, which are blind, rebuild tunnels and arches from both sides of a breach and meet up perfectly in the middle, and they can do this even when the two sides are separated by a large steel plate that is several feet wider and higher than the termitary, placed so that it divides the mound.

Acquired Characteristics Can Be Passed Along

Be all this as it may, what may be mind-blowing about Sheldrake's hypothesis to those accustomed to thinking of heredity as working solely by the passing of genes through egg and sperm is this: acquired characteristics can be passed from one generation to the next. As we know, Dr. Stevenson found that birthmarks and other physiological manifestations often relate to experiences of the remembered past life, particularly when violent death was involved. In my interview with Dr. Tucker, he pointed out that in some situations mental images are known to produce specific effects on the body. For example, some religiously devout individuals develop wounds, called stigmata, which match the crucifixion wounds of Jesus. More than 350 such cases have been reported.

Someone under hypnosis might be told a pencil is a lit cigarette. When the pencil touches that person's arm, a cigarette burn will appear on the arm.

In another case, Dr. Tucker said a man who remembered a traumatic event when he was tied up developed rope marks on his arms. It's amazing what belief and the power of the mind can create.

Let's take a look at the awesome power of belief.

The Power of Belief

The effectiveness of placebos, for example, has been demonstrated time and again in double blind scientific tests. The placebo effect—the phenomenon of patients feeling better after taking dud pills—is seen throughout the field of medicine. One report says that after thousands of studies, hundreds of millions of prescriptions and tens of billions of dollars in sales, sugar pills are as effective at treating depression as antidepressants such as Prozac, Paxil and Zoloft. What's more, placebos cause profound changes in the same areas of the brain affected by these medicines, according to this research. Thoughts and beliefs can and do produce physical changes—in this case in our bodies.

The same research reports that placebos often outperform the medicines they're up against. For example, in a trial conducted in April, 2002, comparing the herbal remedy St. John's wort to Zoloft, St. John's wort fully cured 24 percent of the depressed people who received it. Zoloft cured 25 percent. But the placebo fully cured 32 percent.

Taking what one believes to be real medicine sets up the expectation of results, and what a person expects to happen usually does happen. It's been confirmed, for example, that in cultures where belief exists in voodoo or magic, people will actually die after being cursed by a shaman. It appears such a curse has no power on an outsider who doesn't believe. The expectation causes the result. If you've read my novel, *The Mt. Pelée Redemption,* you know I used this phenomenon as a factor in the plot. In my book, *A Witch in the Family,* I cited this phenomenon as part of what was behind the Salem witch hysteria of 1692. I believe many of the afflicted really did believe witches were tormenting them. Some developed lesions on their skin that looked like teeth marks where they thought witches had bitten them. Others had fits and coughed up blood.

No Wonder Athletes Get Better and Better

The implications of Sheldrake's hypothesis are incredibly widespread. To give an inkling of those falling outside the parameters of this book, consider this: during the past century athletes achieved ever-higher levels of excellence in everything from Olympic track and field to tennis. Improvements in diet, equipment, training techniques and coaching have certainly played a big role, but we must now also consider whether memories located in morphogenetic fields may also be a factor. According to the theory, what has been learned by the pioneers in a sport would become embedded in the morphogenetic field of humanity, and this should make learning the sport, as well as body and muscle coordination, easier for future participants. This might also account for child prodigies and virtuosos. Could it be, for example, that Tiger Woods is the incarnation of a twentieth century golfing great?

Chapter Ten

How Non-Physical Reality May Form the Physical

A non-physical reality is behind and gives rise to the physical world, just as our souls or morphogenetic fields give rise to us. But how does this work?

What I believe to be a plausible indication was given in lectures I came across given by a man named Thomas Troward. He first delivered them at Edinburgh University in Scotland in 1904. Called *The Edinburgh Lectures on Mental Science,* they provide a rationale for how mental images might account for the birthmarks as well as where we exist between lives.

Troward was born in Punjab, India, in 1847 of British parents and went to college in England, but lived most of his life in India. He was a student of metaphysics. He wrote and spoke in a kind of jargon used by nineteenth century scientists. If you have ever tried to read The Origin of Species, for example, you know what I mean. So I translated his lectures into plain, modern English and published them in a book called *How to Master Life* (Oaklea Press, 2015).

Troward believed that underlying everything, the ground of being of all that is, was mind—the medium of thought—and that this is what we experience and see in other living beings and living matter, such as plants and animals, as the life force.

The Phenomenon of Grace

We will explore Troward's theory, but first it is important to understand what I believe is an aspect of the life force. Though not yet recognized by established science, the life force is the direct opposite of entropy—the invisible force that causes things to break down and deteriorate. As such, the life force not only animates the body, it pushes toward growth and evolution as well health and balance in a living organism. Another word for this is grace.

Grace is what happens when the life force or Universal Mind is working in people's lives to insure their growth and development. To the untrained eye, grace appears to be a set of mysterious or unexplainable conditions, events and phenomena that support, nurture, protect or enhance human life and spiritual growth. Grace works in all sorts of ways. The forms of grace seem to be universal. Our immune systems, for example, are tied to it. Modern medicine has only a vague idea why one person exposed to an infectious disease will come down with that disease and another experiencing the same level of exposure will not. On any given day, in practically every public environment, potentially lethal microbes and viruses on surfaces or floating in the air are too numerous to estimate. Yet, most people do not get sick. Why? Doctors would say it is because most people's resistance is fairly high. But what do they really mean? That most people are not run-down or depressed? Perhaps. But not everyone who is run-down and depressed contracts an infectious disease. Yet many do who are perfectly healthy and in good shape. Perhaps those in this category needed a wake up call about something going on in their lives that has them off course—a crises to jog them into reexamining the direction they are headed.

Grace Manifests in Many Ways

The grace of resistance is not limited to infectious disease. Have a chat with a state trooper who has been on the scene of a number of motor vehicle accidents. Ask him what percentage of crashes appeared fatal when he first arrived, and how many actually turned out to be. You're likely to hear some amazing stories of cars or trucks smashed beyond recognition, metal so collapsed, twisted or squashed the trooper will say, "I don't see how anyone could have survived. And yet the person walked away without a scratch," or with only minor injuries. How is it scientifically possible for metal to collapse in such a way as to conform perfectly to the shape of the human body contained inside? Nevertheless, I'm willing to bet the trooper will tell you that this happens more often than not.

When she was about a year old, my now fifteen-year-old daughter bodysurfed down the steep flight of stairs from our kitchen to our basement playroom—not just once, but twice. Another time, a baby sitter turned her back while changing a diaper, and the same daughter rolled off the counter top and fell straight to the bare kitchen floor. Any of these three falls easily could have been fatal. None caused so much as a bruise.

Almost everyone has experienced a close call that could have killed him. One day when I was fourteen, I darted across Jefferson Davis Highway without looking properly. At the time, this was the main north-south highway on the East Coast. This particular stretch had six lanes (three north and three south) with a grass median. A car struck me in midstride. Maybe it was the way the car's bumper caught my foot that lifted me into the air, but I should have been pushed down and run over. Instead, I was lifted up, seemed to fly through the air, and landed on the grass median. The driver was certain I was dead—until I stood up and dusted myself off. I didn't have a scratch. The only evidence of the accident was the stain on my trousers where I'd slid on the grass as I came to a stop. Also, both my shoes were missing. I found them eighty or a hundred feet away where the car had screeched to a halt. If the laws of Newtonian physics had been working that day, I wouldn't be here to put this down on paper.

How, physically, was I lifted into the air? Were angels responsible? I cannot say. But whatever happened, the phenomenon called grace came to my aid, and I lived to be an adult. As a result, I grew and studied and learned enough to enable me to write this book.

Grace Even Uses the IRS

Let me give another example. A few years ago, a friend in one of my Bible study groups and his wife quit their full time jobs in order to attend seminary together. They both had to work part-time and even then were only able to bring in enough to just get by. Unexpected bills arrived, as they always do. They totaled $578, money they simply didn't have. The couple's bank balance registered zero. They had no place to turn. Creditors were calling. Our group prayed that the money they needed would come to them. My friend and his wife prayed, too, as did others.

Two days later, the couple received an envelope in the mail from the IRS saying that their petition had been reviewed. Their tax return from two years prior had been found to be in error. Along with this notice, was a check to them for $588.

Good timing? True. But the amazing thing was, the couple had not filed a petition. Nor had they filed an amended return. Somehow or other, the IRS had done this recalculation on its own. The couple rummaged in their files and pulled out their return from two years prior. The IRS was correct. They found the error that had been referenced.

In my experience, the IRS is not in the mode of helping people out this way. It was grace that brought them that check because they needed the money to stay in school. Seminary was helping them grow, and their growth and the degrees they would receive would someday allow them to help others grow as well.

Why was the check for ten dollars more than they needed? Maybe, since our group met at a restaurant over breakfast on Thursday mornings, grace wanted to pick up the tab.

Troward's Theory Explained

Let's turn back to Thomas Troward's theory. It will help to begin by considering the difference between what we think of as "dead" matter and something we recognize as alive. A plant, such as a sunflower, has a quality that sets it apart from a piece of steel. The sunflower will turn toward the sun under its own power. When first picked, it possesses a kind of glow. This quality Troward called the life force. On the other hand, the piece of steel appears totally inert. Yet we know that at the quantum level, the steel is alive with motion. Quantum physicists tell us motion or energy is what comprises all matter. Atoms and molecules are energy. Vibrations. Many believe the universe is alive—a living thing. When the physicist, Henry P. Stapp, was on my radio show in summer, 2008, I asked him about this. He confirmed the widely held view by quantum physicists that the universe resembles a giant thinker. I have come to picture the universe as the thought of an infinitely vast mind of organizing intelligence.

Let's get back to the sunflower. By outward appearances it is alive, and the steel is not. Few would argue this. But one might argue that a plant's state of "aliveness" is not the same as an animal's. Consider the difference in aliveness between a sunflower, an earthworm, and a goldfish. Each appears to be progressively more alive.

Now, let's add a dog, a three year old child, and a stand up comedian on the Tonight Show. Each has a progressively higher level of intelligence. So, to some extent, what we call the degree of "aliveness" can be measured by the amount of awareness or intelligence displayed—in other words, by the power of thought.

As stated before, I believe mind underlies and creates the entire universe. It's everywhere—the ground of being. But it becomes more evident to us—we can see it more clearly—as it becomes more self-aware. From Troward's point of view, "mind," "spirit" and "life"—or the life force—are one and the same, the distinctive quality of which is thought. He argued that the distinctive quality of matter, as in the piece of steel, is form.

Form implies the occupation of space and also limitation within certain boundaries. Thought (or life) implies neither. When we think of thought or life as existing in any particular form we associate it with the idea of occupying space, so that an elephant may be said to consist of a vastly larger amount of living substance than a mouse. But if we think of life as the fact of "aliveness," or animating spirit, we do not associate it with occupying space. The mouse is quite as much alive as the elephant, notwithstanding the difference in size. For

Troward this was an important point. If we can conceive of anything as not occupying space, or as having no form, it must be present in its totality anywhere and everywhere—that is to say, at every point of space simultaneously.

The fact of thought being everywhere or non local was demonstrated by Stephan A. Schwartz, whose remote viewing seminar class, as you recall from an earlier chapter, correctly identified the location and circumstances of Saddam Hussein's capture.

Schwartz conducted another experiment that demonstrates mind is everywhere at once, and that thoughts are not electromagnetic waves. Thoughts are in the single mind we, everything and everyone, shares. His experiment proves telepathy does not work by electromagnetic waves being sent and received like a walky-talky or radio and TV, but rather, that mind and thought are ubiquitous.

To conduct this experiment Schwartz had researchers lowered in a submarine to a water depth below which has been proven that electromagnetic waves—regardless of their frequency or strength—simply cannot penetrate. Accomplished remote viewers in the submarine got the same results about targets on the surface as did remoter viewers on the surface.

ESP / telepathy experiments were also conducted. Results between those in the sub and those on the surface were in no way diminished from what had been the case when all were located on the surface. Telepathy was thus demonstrated to be disassociated with electromagnetic waves.

In other words, ESP does not work by messages traveling from one mind to another because, as I have been saying, there is only one mind. The messages don't have to travel. All are part of it.

We and everything are aspects of this mind. What mystics have been saying for millennia is correct: All Is One. Being in a submarine deep below the surface of the ocean doesn't change this.

The details of this experiment can be found in Schwartz's book, *OPENING TO THE INFINITE: The Art and Science of Nonlocal Awareness* (Nemoseen Media, 2007).

The implications are difficult to wrap our thoughts around, but true. Mind does not occupy space, and it transcends time. This is how remote viewers could learn the facts of Saddam Hussein's capture months in advance, and predict the time and place Skylab would fall to earth.

The bottom line is that all mind, the life force, must exist everywhere at once in a universal here and an everlasting now.

More Evidence Mind Is Ubiquitous

The evidence clearly indicates mind—life force—is the primal stuff of the universe. This can be seen by observing nature. Consider a sunflower. It has no brain. According to currently accepted science, it can have no awareness. But it does have awareness. It turns its face to the sun, and it follows the sun across the sky from sunrise to dusk.

This requires some form of awareness.

Living plants are aware. Scientifically constructed, double blind experiments by researchers, including theoretical biophysicist of the University of Marburg in Germany, Fritz-Albert Popp, have demonstrated this.* And this isn't news. About 40 years ago a fellow named Cleve Backster demonstrated plants are aware by using polygraph machines. In Backster's most famous experiment, he hooked up plants in his office suite to polygraph machines, then set up a device to randomly dump a cup of living brine shrimp into a pot of boiling water. The needles on the polygraph machines would go wild each time the shrimp hit the water and went to their deaths. The plants were picking up their distress and demise.

But what led Cleve Backster to construct and carry out this experiment may be even more of an eye-opener. Lynne McTaggart, author of *The Field: The Quest for the Secret Force of the Universe,* told the following story on my show early in 2008.

Backster was and is an expert on polygraph machines and their operation—in other words, lie detectors. One evening about 40 years ago when Backster was a young man, he was sitting in his office with nothing much to do. His eyes fell on an office plant and he had an idea. He decided to hook up one of his machines to the plant and see if he could get it to react. He connected the machine and poured a glass of water into the soil around the plant. Nothing happened. The polygraph registered boredom.

Backster started thinking about what he might do to get a reaction out of the plant, and he had an idea.

"I think I'll burn one of its leaves."

At that moment, the polygraph machine went wild. The plant had reacted to his thought! The more Backster thought about burning the plant, the more the needle on the polygraph machine went ballistic.

Cleve Backster conducted many experiments along these lines which are described in his book, *Primary Perception: Bio Communication with Plants, Living Foods, and Human Cells* (White Rose Millennium Press, 2003).

People who have what's called green thumbs may think it is because they send kind thoughts to their plants. It may be true that kind thoughts help make happy plants, but as we now know, thoughts are not sent and received. Thoughts just are—part of the mind we and everything and everyone share.

Mind Creates Matter

Troward's theory would have to be taken seriously by the scientific community if it could be demonstrated mind can produce matter.

Well, you know what? It has been demonstrated. I referenced the following case in my book, *Amazin Truth*. It comes from Stephen Braude, the University of Maryland philosophy professor whose work was discussed earlier in this book. In one of my interviews with with him, we discussed his book,

Life After Death

The Gold Leaf Lady and Other Parapsychological Investigations (The University of Chicago Press, 2007).

It's about Katie, a woman born in Tennessee, the tenth of twelve children. She is apparently a simple woman. Illiterate, she lives in Florida with her husband and works as a domestic. She is also a psychic who has had documented successes helping the police solve crimes. In one instance, she was able to describe the details of the case so thoroughly and accurately, the police regarded her as a suspect until those actually responsible were apprehended.

She also apports objects—in other words, she somehow causes them to disappear in one place and reappear in another. And that's not all. Seeds reportedly germinate rapidly in her cupped hands. Observers claim to have seen her bend metal, and she is both a healer and a medium or channel. For whatever reason, her share of the life force must be of the high-octane variety.

She cannot read or write in her native English, but she has been video taped writing quatrains in medieval French similar both in style and content to the actual quatrains of Nostradamus. But most amazing is what appears spontaneously on her skin—on her hands, face, arms, legs, back—apparently out of thin air. It looks like gold leaf, a thin version of the wrapping of a Hersey's Kiss.

Katie cannot control when this happens, but Dr. Braude and other witnesses have seen the foil materialize firsthand. Dr. Braude actually video taped it appearing. He has also taken the foil to be analyzed. It turns out not to be gold at all, but brass—approximately 80 percent copper and 20 percent zinc.

Katie's Unconscious Mind Creates Brass Foil

Think about this. Her mind causes the foil to materialize. There is no other plausible explanation. In fact, Dr. Braude believes she produces brass rather than gold for a reason—albeit a subconscious one. Katie has a very difficult and tense relationship with her husband. Once she apported a carving set. It just appeared. And her husband—apparently nonplussed—said, "So what? It's not worth anything."

Soon afterward, gold colored foil began appearing on Katie's skin. But it wasn't gold, it was fool's gold—brass. Dr. Braude thinks this is how she gets back at him.

Katie doesn't know how her mind is able to make brass out of what appears to be nothing. She probably doesn't consciously know why it's brass and not some other substance. But nonetheless, her mind does it—the mind of which we all are part. Have I said it using these words, already? Everything is created by mind. Everything is mind.

Two Kinds of Thought, Lower and Higher

How does this help us understand how there can be life between lives, and how those children got the birthmarks?

First, Troward would point out that there are two kinds

of thought. We might call them lower and higher, or subjective and objective because what differentiates the higher from the lower is the recognition of self. A plant, a worm, and perhaps a goldfish possess the lower kind only. They are unaware of self. Perhaps a dog, and certainly a boy and a comedian possess both. The higher variety of self-aware thought is possessed in progressively larger amounts as if ascending a scale.

Troward believed the lower mode of thought, the subjective, is the subconscious intelligence—or mind—present everywhere that, among other things, supports and controls the mechanics of life in every species and in every individual. It causes plants to grow toward the sun and to push roots into the soil. It causes hearts to beat and lungs to take in air without our having to think about it. This ubiquitous subjective mind controls all of the so-called involuntary functions of the body.

That this lower kind of thought is everywhere at once coincides with Carl Jung's theory that we humans share a Universal Mind. Moreover, we each have our own portion, our individual subconscious mind that blends into the collective mind. We also have a conscious mind, the producer of objective thought that makes us self-aware. The two types of mind are inextricably linked in that our conscious mind arises out of the subconscious and remains linked to it. The gradual emergence of self-aware thought out of the universal subconscious mind over the course of evolution is implicit in our consideration of the plant, earthworm, goldfish, dog, boy, comedian and so forth up the scale.

Our conscious minds are an aspect of our individual morphogenetic field hypothesized by Rupert Sheldrake, and our individual field is part of the larger field of our particular birth family. Genes determine our hair and skin color and the color of our eyes, but our family's morphogenetic field determines the form our bodies take, such as the shapes of our noses and our ears. The field of our family is in turn part of the morphogenetic field of humankind, and so on up the ladder to include all living things, Gaia—the earth, and ultimately, the universe.

Who are we? In each life we are a combination of the conscious mind or soul that carries over from previous lives, the genes and morphogenetic field of the family we are born into, and the environment into which we were born and raised. More fundamentally, we are sparks of the Universal Mind experiencing itself.

How the Reincarnates Got Their Birthmarks

How can we be born missing a limb we lost in the previous life or with birthmarks that mimic the wound we died from? As Troward believed, our conscious or objective mind must have power over the subjective mind. This can be seen in the phenomenon of hypnosis, which works because the hypnotist bypasses his subject's conscious mind and speaks directly to his subject's subconscious (subjective) mind. The subconscious has no choice but to bring into reality that which is communicated directly to it as fact by a conscious mind.

Being totally subjective, the subconscious mind cannot step outside of itself for an objective look. The result is that the subconscious (subjective) mind is entirely under the control of the conscious (objective) mind. As a result, the subconscious will work diligently to support or to bring into reality whatever the conscious mind believes to be true. A person's subjective mind must be at work as his fetus grows. The result is that if we believe we have missing fingers, a leg or a hand, we will be missing a leg, a hand or fingers, when we are born.

The implications of this are staggering. As many have been saying for quite some time, our beliefs literally create our personal realities.

Here's some advice. Next time you are between lives, if you have lost some body part in the life just past, think yourself a new one before you reincarnate. Or take the time to process the life just past, and resist the temptation to return to the physical realm too quickly.

Get Ready for Pseudo Skeptics to Throw up Flak

While I believe Julie Beischel's work combines with that of Bruce Greyson, Ian Stevenson, Jim Tucker and others reported upon in this book to form an airtight case for the continuation of consciousness, I am equally certain the pseudo skeptics will continue to hold onto and profess the view that death is the end. I expect they will do so even though there are no dangling straws for them to grasp.

I believe this to be the case for two reasons. The first has to do with self-preservation. Some of these skeptics have, perhaps unwittingly, been teaching classes and writing books full of erroneous information for years. Throwing the old paradigm on the trash heap of history may likewise place them and their reputations on the trash heap.

The second is that some may have good reason to want to believe consciousness does not continue. These folks may be afraid they will be judged after death. Because of this, they may prefer to remain in a state of denial.

They should not, however, fear the judgment of others. Those who have had near death experiences report the only judging done during the life review is by the individual undergoing the review. Others present at the review may offer advice or solace, but they heed Jesus' command: "Do not judge or you too will be judged." (Matthew 7:1)

Of course, it's true we can be harsher judges of ourselves than impartial observers might be. I for one am guilty of things in my youth I'm not looking forward to reviewing.

But, when all is said and done, think of the good the realization consciousness lives on will do. At last we will come to the realization we are eternal. Think how that will change someone who now thinks otherwise. It's got to make him or her see the world differently.

How Will Knowing You Are Eternal Change You?

How about you? What will you do differently now that you know?

No longer will it be necessary to fear death—unless you are worried about your judgment of yourself. But now that you know, you can do something about it. Find the people you harmed and make amends. And change your life: "Give to the poor and you will have treasure in heaven." (Matthew 19:21)

You no longer have to feel the great sense of loss you may have felt in the past when someone you love dies. You will see them again.

You can chuck the mid-life crises, knowing you will have the opportunity for another go at youth in a future life.

We can all come to view death for what many have long believed it to be: a transition, rather than the end.

No longer will it be viewed as a particularly good idea to keep someone alive artificially on life support, who has no chance to recover, and is suffering.

And consider this. Pregnant women are taught how to give birth. It will likewise make sense for everyone to learn how to die as comfortably as possible. It will also make sense to teach people what to expect when they do.

Look for the light. Go to it.

Chapter Eleven
Why Accepting the Truth Can Be Difficult

Why is it so difficult for some of us to believe in life after death? We have discussed why some skeptics may never give up their position, but what about those who would like to believe but cannot bring themselves to do so?

I'd say a main reason is that it's hard to shake off what one has been taught since kindergarten. The science of life we learned in school is based on an erroneous tenet—that consciousness and intelligence came about as results of evolution. The truth is the other way around. Evolution came about as a result of consciousness and intelligence.

A quick summary of what we were taught goes like this: First RNA, then DNA came along. This happened by accident. One celled animals formed in the sea and became more complex over time as traits developed that helped them survive. Random mutations produced ever more complex organisms that won the battles for survival. The fittest were able to propagate and pass on their genes. Eventually, some crawled out of the sea and evolution continued on land. Brains—which had happened by accident and gave their owners big advantages over the brainless—became more complex and created awareness and intelligence.

In a nutshell, that's what we learned. But it seems more logical, given what we now know, that consciousness and intelligence came first and are the bedrock of all that is. Evolution was helped along by grace, which is a phenomenon of the life force, or ground of being.

Let me tell you what makes sense to me based on everything we know that's been set down in this book up to now.

In the beginning only one consciousness existed—only one mind. Now, many separate consciousnesses exist. Sentient beings have their own unique consciousness as a result of evolution.

Consciousness is not caused by electrons jumping across synapses. Consciousness just is. Some of it became separated into unique souls as morphogenetic fields formed in the primal consciousness, or ground of being. This ground of being is the clay evolution molded into who we are—a result of the long journey up from RNA, DNA, and the first sparks of consciousness that formed one celled creatures in the sea.

Mystics refer to sparks being cast out from the Tao or godhead. They are referring to the differentiated consciousness of these morphogenetic fields. Primitive morphogenetic fields became more and more complex over time as they adapted to their environments in their quest for growth and survival. As the millennia passed, portions of the ground of being of consciousness evolved objective awareness.

Parenthetically, this may be how the universe reproduces itself— sort of like an amoeba dividing and subdividing and dividing again. Even though we are separate, however, we nonetheless remain connected to and part of the ground of being from which we came—just as a TV channel remains part of the complete ban of TV channel frequencies.

Our bodily senses make us feel separate. These are necessary, of course, for us to function in the physical realm. We need them to operate our bodies. In the East the sense of separation is seen as an illusion created by the senses called "Maya."

Created in the Likeness of Our Creator

Consciousness, the ground of being, is the bedrock of all that is. But for it to enter into and experience physical reality requires a brain and a body. Once encapsulated in a body, consciousness experiences primarily through the focal point of the brain via the medium of eyes, ears, sense of smell, taste and touch. It seems this nexus is where consciousness is located. In a way it is, but remote viewing and retrieval of information through psychic means are still possible because we remain at all times part of the one mind. Sentient beings are focal points of consciousness within the larger consciousness, and some can access information from the larger, ocean of consciousness. This is because all is connected. All is one.

Mystics have been saying "All Is One" for millennia. On my radio show, I have had a number of people describe the experience of spontaneously realizing this. For some it was brought about when they were out in nature and experienced a sunrise or a sunset. For others it happened at the birth of a child, or as a result of a near death experience.

In his book, The Rebirth of Nature, *The Greening of Science and God,* Rupert Sheldrake quotes a woman, an art teacher, who recounted an experience she had while walking on the Pangbourne Moors at the age of five. She puts into words what I believe many of us have felt at one time or another but perhaps later dismissed when our "rational" minds again got the upper hand:

Suddenly I seemed to see the mist as a shimmering gossamer tissue and the harebells, appearing here and there, seemed to shine with a brilliant fire. Somehow I understood that this was the living tissue of life itself, in which all that we call consciousness is embedded, appearing here and there as a shining focus of energy in the more diffused whole. In that moment I knew that I had my special place, as had all other things, animate and so-called inanimate, and that we were all part of this universal tissue which was both fragile yet immensely strong, and utterly good and beneficent.

Until now, people came to the realization of oneness and that life is eternal through an epiphany, as happened above. Now there are facts—the facts set down in this book—that make it possible to come to the realization through logic. How quickly an individual comes to this will depend, I believe, on his or her personality type. I will attempt to explain.

Life After Death

The Myers-Briggs personality approach has four dimensions:

I or E (Introspective versus Extroverted)

N or S (Intuition versus Sensation as a preference for information gathering and decision making, i.e., Intuitive versus Sensible—sensible in the strict meaning of the word as in perceiving through the senses.)

T or F (Thinking or Feeling)

J or P (Judging or Perceiving)

My personality type is INTJ. So I'm introspective, prefer intuition, like to use rational thought rather than feelings when considering things, and I'm constantly judging stuff rather than passively perceiving it. One way this manifests is that what makes sense to me is much more important than who said it. Some people don't like having me around because of this—my cross to bear. They have the feeling I see through them, like the little boy who shouted, "The king has no clothes!" while everyone else was thinking, "The king must have clothes. After all, he's the king. It must be me who just can't see them."

Less than two percent of the population is like me. Every personality type has its good points and unique abilities. We INTJs are known as builders of theoretical models. We see life as a giant chess game—understanding it and winning simply require arranging the pieces properly.

Of the four dimensions, the N versus S is the largest source of misunderstandings and hard feelings. The intuitive person often finds complex ideas coming to him as a complete whole. It is then up to him or her to reverse engineer these ideas in order to determine why they are true. Sensibles go at things from the other direction, which means they are likely to want more data than an intuitive will think necessary.

Ian Stevenson may have been a Sensible. He collected and verified more than 2500 reports of children's memories of past lives. An Intuitive, having soon recognized a pattern, would have stopped after investigating and verifying a dozen or so. The main reason to collect more would be to convince the Sensibles. Of course, this may be why Stevenson did so.

Only 25 percent of the population is Intuitive. The big majority, 75 percent, are Sensibles. It seems to me 2500 confirmed cases ought to be enough to convince even the most ardent Sensible.

How about you? Are you convinced? If not, there may be another reason. Let's look into that one.

People Are Hardwired to Not Change Their Minds

Sensibles aren't the only ones who don't change their minds easily when presented with new information. People are not easily swayed who already have a hard and fast opinion about the way things are. This has been demonstrated through scientific research.

For years, Drew Westen, a psychologist at Emory University, has been studying how people think, particularly in the area of politics. For my money, those who hold steadfastly to the old ideas of materialism in the face of data indicating a universe made of something we can't see are much like members of a political party who refuse to see where their own party or candidate has veered off track.

In experiments using MRI scans, Westen has demonstrated that persons with partisan preferences believe what they want to believe regardless of the facts. Not only that, they unconsciously congratulate themselves—the reward centers of their brains light up—when they reject new information that does not square with their predetermined views.

In one test, subjects were presented with contradictory statements made by George Bush and John Kerry. Republicans judged Kerry's flip-flop harshly, while letting Bush off the hook for his. Democrats did the reverse. Interestingly, brain scans showed that the parts of the brain accounting for emotion were far more active during the experiment than the reasoning parts.

Anyone who follows politics will not be surprised by this. The truth is, Westen's research does not relate anything new. Solzhenitsyn characterized this phenomenon as "the desire not to know." In 1915 George Santayana acknowledged in a letter to his sister that "when I read [newspapers] I form perhaps a new opinion of the newspaper but seldom a new opinion on the subject discussed." Westen's research has value because it backs up impressions with empirical facts—brain scans.

In another experiment Westen conducted before the 2004 presidential election, participants were told a soldier at Abu Ghraib was charged with torturing prisoners and wanted to subpoena Bush administration officials. Different participants were given different amounts of evidence supporting the soldier's claim that he had been told the administration had suspended Geneva Convention rules regarding treatment of prisoners. But it didn't matter how much information they had.

Westen said, "Eighty-four percent of the time, we could predict whether people believed the evidence was sufficient to subpoena Donald Rumsfeld based on just three things: the extent to which they liked Republicans, the extent to which they liked human rights groups like Amnesty International, and the extent to which they liked the U.S. military."

Results such as this might help explain why some debates never seem to end. People are invested in the positions they take. So, as Westen puts it, they have a tendency to weigh not just the facts, but also, "what they would feel if they came to one conclusion or another, and they often come to the conclusion that would make them feel better, no matter what the facts are."

Now that you know this, I hope you will set anything you learned in school or elsewhere aside, and truly consider what's presented in this book.

Chapter Twelve
High Time for a Paradigm Shift

One reason it's hard to accept that consciousness continues after death is that it requires scrapping the materialistic model of the world most of us still hold. But it's important to understand models are just that—approximations of how things are. This chapter will explain how the current model developed. The chapter that follows will offer a new one into which the continuation of consciousness fits comfortably.

Whether we realize it or not, we each have a worldview—or a model of how things work. You might think of this as a stack of cans that forms a pyramid you might see as a grocery store aisle end display. Each can represents an individual belief. Each belief in the display supports other beliefs. Try to change a foundational belief, and the whole thing may come tumbling down. That's why I will offer you an entirely new model of the world so you can replace the whole thing at once.

As we will soon see, in the past century scientists have been presented with information that would require tearing down and rebuilding from the ground up the model they hold of reality. Rather than do so, most have taken the easy way by dismissing as anomalies information that does not fit. We saw in the last chapter that this reaction is common. If enough of these so-called anomalies build up, however, they can be like water backing up behind a dam. Eventually, that dam has to burst. I believe that time has come.

Let's start by taking a look at how we got to the worldview, or model, that's about to be washed downstream.

A Very Old World View

There was a time, anthropologists tell us, when humans felt at one with nature. This can still be seen today in primitive cultures. Called pantheism, humans felt they were an integral part of the ecosystem. The Divine showed itself in many forms and was present in all things.

But as humans grew more self aware, they began to feel separation. The myth of Adam and Eve recalls the time when humans parted company with the view that they could commune with the Divine. They cut the cord by exercising free will.

No longer seeing God in themselves and in others, we humans conjured up gods outside ourselves. In ancient Greece, for example, many gods representing various human qualities were thought to exist. The worldview that evolved in those ancient times had man in the middle between two worlds—a place the Chinese referred to as the Middle Kingdom. The gods lived above the clouds of Mt. Olympus, although they did come to earth now and then, mostly to cause problems for humans.

Below the Middle Kingdom—what caused it to be in the middle—was the underworld, home of the dead, where Hades was in charge and the three-headed dog Cereberus guarded a gate one got to after crossing the River Styx.

Different cultures had different takes on this three-layered universe. Then as now, ideas about God and gods differed depending on the group one belonged to. The Egyptians had Bal. The Jews had the god of Abraham. The Romans and the Greeks had a pantheon full.

The Idea of One God Created a New World View

Then came Jesus of Nazareth and the idea emerged that only one God ruled over creation—although He did have angels and eventually saints who took up some of the positions left vacant by departing Roman and Greek gods.

In 1994 Karen Armstrong published a book, *A History of God*, that chronicled history of the emergence of the concept of one God.

Because of this idea, the worldview changed somewhat. God and angels replaced the pantheon of gods above the clouds. A fallen angel, Satan, replaced Hades. The place below the ground became hell rather than the underworld—where evildoers went. The good folk would be raised at the end of time on judgment day and given new, light bodies.

This view held sway for better than a thousand years but was destined to change again because of a new scientific discovery by Christopher Columbus (1451-1506).

Columbus lived on high ground overlooking a Mediterranean harbor. I have visited the ruin of what is said to be the house where he grew up. In that part of the world there is almost no humidity and the air is very clear. If Columbus had good eyes, he would not even have needed a spyglass to see ships climb up over the horizon as they approached the harbor. I've witnessed this myself. Columbus could see the world was round and he must have decided to prove it by sailing west to get to the spice islands of the East Indies.

Columbus never realized it himself, but he didn't actually get there. Nevertheless, some of Ferdinand Magellan's (1480-1521) crew did, and beyond. Of the 237 men who set out on five ships in 1519, 18 actually completed the circumnavigation of the globe and returned to Spain in 1522.

The newly realized fact that the world was round forced the then commonly held world view to change. Nevertheless, since people and, most important, Church leaders believed that God had created it, the earth remained at the center of the universe. Now heaven, the dwelling place of God, was seen as being somewhere above the stars. Hell was still beneath the ground, down where it was hot, the place from which molten lava spewed when volcanoes erupted.

The World View Gets an Update

It wasn't long before this world view had to be updated. A fellow named Nicolaus Copernicus (1473-1543) determined the sun was at the center of the solar system. But the Church—the authority back then as science is today—pretty much ignored this concept because it did not go along with accepted canon. This "look the other way" tactic will be seen time and again in the twentieth century.

Then, a century later, along came Galileo Galilei (1564-1642), a man who would not leave well enough alone. Galileo—among other things an astronomer—championed Copernicus's assertion as proven fact. As a result, Galileo started having to watch his back. This was heresy. At that time people were being burned at the stake for less. Indeed, the leaders of the Church told Galileo he'd better recant, and he did. As a result, Galileo got off easy, spending the final years of his life under house arrest on orders of the Inquisition.

But even the Church couldn't keep word from getting out. Gradually, the accepted views of the day began to change.

A Tiny World Comes into View

In 1675, a Dutchman named Antoni van Leeuwenhoek (1632-1723) —an amateur lens grinder and microscope builder—saw for the first time tiny organisms he called "animalcules" living in stagnant water. He also spotted them in scum collected from his teeth. Leeuwenhock didn't know or even speculate that "animalcules" might cause disease. It took until the nineteenth century for that revelation to dawn. At the time, the idea creatures so small they were invisible to the naked eye entered the body to make a person sick and sometimes die would have seemed totally absurd. It was thought demons and the devil caused such things, or that God did it to punish sinners. In 1692 in Salem, MA, 18 were hanged and one was crushed to death because they were thought to be witches in league with Satan. No wonder after that, and down until today, the idea of Satan and demons and witchcraft was thought to be pure superstition. To believe in such things was to invite witch hunts and mass hysteria, and nobody wanted that.

The Age of Reason Dawns

Even so, a new day was dawning, a period alternately referred to as "The Age of Enlightenment" and "The Age of Reason." English philosopher, Thomas Hobbes (1588-1679), had argued that aside from God—the "first cause" who created the material world—nothing existed that is not of the material world. The logic he used was simple. How could it if God created everything?

This view was ultimately to lead to the great clock maker theory, the idea that God created the universe, wound it up, let it go, and was no longer involved in its operation. Natural laws also had been created that kept going what had been set in motion. Called Deism, many founding fathers, including my personal hero, Thomas Jefferson, subscribed to this view. Jefferson, by the way, was an INTJ.

Hobbes had a big impact on the Age of Enlightenment, which was to pick up steam in the eighteenth century. But the big kahuna was Sir Isaac Newton (1643 – 1727), an English physicist, mathematician, astronomer, natural philosopher, alchemist, and theologian. Certainly one of the most influential men of all time, his *Philosophiæ Naturalis Principia Mathematica,* published in 1687, is considered to be the groundwork for most of classical mechanics. Newton described universal gravitation and the three laws of motion that dominated the scientific view of the physical universe at least until the advent of quantum mechanics. It seems safe to say Thomas Hobbes's materialistic view of reality coupled with Newton's mechanistic view is the bedrock of scientific thinking today, except among quantum physicists.

The prevailing worldview that emerged from the Age of Reason was that the universe might be compared to a giant machine. The Sun was at the center of the solar system. The Earth and planets revolved around it. Nothing existed but the material world. What was thought of in the seventeenth century and before as the invisible world of spirit did not exist. Everything that happened had a logical cause. Natural laws governed everything.

Darwin's Theory Takes Hold

In 1859 an Englishman, Charles Darwin, published On the Origin of Species, a seminal work in scientific literature and a landmark work in evolutionary biology. Its full title, *On the Origin of Species by Means of Natural Selection, or the Preservation of Favoured Races in the Struggle for Life,* uses the term "races" to mean biological varieties. Darwin's book introduced the theory that populations evolve over the course of generations through a process of natural selection. It presented a body of evidence indicating the diversity of life arose through a branching pattern of evolution and common descent. In other words, God had not created the variety of life on the planet, nor had He created humans. All this had happened through a natural—what might be seen as mechanical—process. This became accepted as fact among the educated classes.

But astute scientists then and now realized something important was missing from Darwin's theory. It cannot be reconciled with the second law of thermodynamics, or Law of Entropy—the fact that in a closed system things tend to break down and fall apart, rather than get better. In other words, your old car is not going to get better by itself. It's going to require outside help, meaning you are going to have to write a check or pull out a credit card.

How then could life get more complex by accident? What caused an eye, a kidney, a heart, ears, and all those complex systems to develop? We can guess from the theories outlined in this book it has something to do with the life force—the underlying intelligence, subjective mind, push-me pull-me effect coupled with grace. That's now. But only Thomas Troward considered such things back then. Most ignored his theory and overlooked the flaw. Many still do today.

Darwin's theories reinforced the rationalist idea that the so called supernatural was a figment of human imagination and—not wanting to be burned at the stake—most scientists probably wanted to keep it safely buried. Life and its diversity were results of a natural process known as survival of the fittest coupled with the environment in which a particular species had evolved. Intelligence and mind had evolved as life had evolved and had reached its pinnacle in humans. Mind and intelligence were produced by an organ, the brain, which had resulted from this evolution. Thought was created by the brain and would later be envisioned as being a result of electrons jumping across synapses. It was contained within the skull. ESP was impossible and so was magic.

A Wedge Is Driven Between Science and Religion

With this worldview, a wedge was inserted and hammered in between science, religion and any possibility of things so called supernatural. Hobbes had said nothing existed but the physical. If this were so, where could God possibly reside? What about the heavenly hosts? Thought was contained within the skull so what possible good could prayer do?

A line was drawn. Educated men and women could not believe in God and prayer or angels or ghosts and demons, which were seen as figments of ignorance and superstition. Many may have had a yearning for God—as humans seem to for the spiritual—but could not rationalize His existence. All were forced to choose between religion and science, though many attempted to straddle the line—as they still do today.

Now, in the early part of the twenty-first century, this worldview continues to be the only socially acceptable one in some circles. But there are signs it is beginning to crumble. Hundreds of thousands, perhaps millions, have shifted to a new world view based on a new branch of science called quantum mechanics and the findings of scientific research that do not fit the materialist-reductionist mold. I hope this book will do its part to knock that view down once and for all.

Let's look at some of the pioneers who have not been afraid to speak out, as well as their ideas and discoveries that conflict with the prevailing nineteenth-twentieth century worldview. The following does not in any way represent an exhaustive list. My apologies to anyone who feels left out, and to anyone who thinks I have overlooked a key figure.

Matter = Energy

In 1905, Albert Einstein (1879-1955), a German-born theoretical physicist, published a paper proving that light behaves both as a wave and as particles. This, as well as Einstein's famous formula, $E = MC^2$, indicates reality and matter are not what they seem. Matter or mass as it is referred to in this formula is equivalent to energy and vice versa.

In 1912 Swiss psychiatrist Carl Jung (1875-1961) published *Wandlungen und Symbole der Libido* (known in English as The Psychology of the Unconscious) that postulated a collective unconscious, sometimes known as collective subconscious. According to Jung there is an unconscious mind shared by a society, a people, or all humanity, that is the product of ancestral experience and contains such concepts as the classic archetypes, science, religion, and morality.

Quantum physicists came along who expanded on Einstein's work. Niels Henrik David Bohr, a Danish physicist, made fundamental contributions to understanding atomic structure and quantum mechanics, for which he received the Nobel Prize in Physics in 1922. He is quoted as having said, "Everything we call real is made of things that cannot be regarded as real."

Nothing is really solid. Everything is energy—vibrations.

ESP and Psycho Kinesis Are Proven Real

As we know from our earlier discussion, in the early 1930s a man named J. B. (Joseph Banks) Rhine moved from Harvard University to Duke to set up a parapsychology laboratory. Rhine not only founded the parapsychology lab at Duke, he also founded the Journal of Parapsychology and the Foundation for Research on the Nature of Man. His double blind studies conducted largely between 1930 and 1960 established that ESP exists and is real. Not mentioned in our earlier discussion, they also showed psycho kinesis—mind over matter—is real as well, at least to a small degree.

His findings were either scoffed at or ignored by the scientific community then as they continue to be today.

Zen Is Introduced to the West

In 1953, Eugen Herrigel (1884-1955), a German philosopher who taught philosophy at Tohoku Imperial University in Sendai, Japan, from 1924-1929 published the book, Zen and the Art of Archery. This introduced Zen Buddhism to the West and the concept that "All Is One," i.e., everything is connected rather than made up of separate parts. How else could Zen masters shoot arrows while blindfolded and consistently hit the bull's-eyes of targets many yards away?

In 1966 a British philosopher named Alan Watts (1915-1973) published a book called *The Book: On the Taboo Against Knowing Who You Are* that went into detail about Buddhist thought. Known as an interpreter and popularizer of Asian philosophies for a Western audience, Watts wrote more than 25 books and numerous articles on subjects such as personal identity, the true nature of reality, higher consciousness and the meaning of life. His writings and ideas fueled a new movement which came to be known as New Age.

Plants Tune into Thoughts

As discussed, a polygraph expert named Cleve Backster (born 1924) began research in 1966 that demonstrated living plants tune into the thoughts and intentions of humans as well as other aspects of their environments, thus indicating some sort of hidden mental connection between living things.

His findings were ridiculed, but have since been confirmed by other researchers.

In 1978 a young man with a B.A., M.A., and Ph.D. from the University of Virginia and an M.D. from Georgia Medical School named Raymond Moody (born 1944) published a book called *Life After Life,* in which he detailed the experiences of people who had been clinically dead and resuscitated.

The Phenomenon of Grace Is Publicized

Also in 1978, a psychiatrist named M. Scott Peck (1936-2005) published a book that became a huge bestseller called, *The Road Less Travelled: A New Psychology Of Love, Traditional Values And Spiritual Growth.* Among other things, Peck's book dealt with the phenomenon of grace, which we covered in the last chapter. He said grace was both common and to a certain extent, predictable. He also wrote that, "grace will remain unexplainable within the conceptual framework of conventional science and 'natural law' as we understand it."

Grace is the unseen force that brings the best possible results out of unfortunate events and circumstances, .i.e., "every cloud has a silver lining." In Peck's own words, "There is a force, the mechanism of which we do not fully understand, that seems to operate routinely in most people to protect and encourage their physical health even under the most adverse conditions." His book gives specific examples.

It seems to me, grace is the life force at work.

Quantum Physics Is Introduced to the Masses

In 1979, Gary Zukav, a former Green Beret during the war in Vietnam, published a book called the Dancing *Wu Li Masters: An Overview of the New Physics.* Targeted for laymen, it explained the basics of quantum physics in everyday language, i.e., without the use of complicated mathematics. Zukav concluded that "the philosophical implication of quantum mechanics is that all of the things in our universe (including us) that appear to exist independently are actually parts of one all-encompassing organic pattern, and that no parts of that pattern are ever really separate from it or from each other."

Also in 1979, James Lovelock published a book called *Gaia: A New Look at Life on Earth* that explained his idea that life on earth functions as a single organism. In contrast to the conventional belief that living matter is passive in the face of threats to its existence, the book explored the hypothesis that the earth's living matter—air, ocean, and land surfaces—forms a complex system that has the capacity to keep the Earth a fit place for life. Since Gaia was first published, many of Jim Lovelock's predictions have come true.

The Spiritual Dimension Is Explored

In the mid 1980s a television series appeared on PBS called *The Power of Myth,* featuring author and Sarah Lawrence College Comparative Religion Professor, Joseph Campbell (1904-

1987). These programs made an impact on a significant segment of the public and opened their eyes to the possibility of the existence of what might be termed "a spiritual dimension." This can be summed up using Campbell's own words, "Anyone who has had an experience of mystery knows there is a dimension of the universe that is not available to his senses."

Scientific Studies Demonstrate the Efficacy of Prayer

In July, 1988, Dr. Randolph Byrd, a cardiologist, published an article in the Southern Medical Journal about the effects of prayer on cardiac patients. Over a ten-month period, he used a computer to assign 393 patients admitted to the coronary care unit at San Francisco General Hospital either to a group that was prayed for by home prayer groups (192 patients), or to a group that was not prayed for (201). A double blind test, neither the patients, doctors, nor the nurses knew which group a patient was in.

The patients who were remembered in prayer had remarkably, and a statistically significant number of better experiences and outcomes than those who were not prayed for. Also, fewer prayed-for patients died, although the difference between groups in this case was not large enough to be considered statistically significant.

In 1994 Rupert Sheldrake, a British biochemist whose theory has already been discussed, published a book called *A New Science of Life*. The editors of the British journal, Nature, called this book, "the best candidate for burning there has been for many years."

Researchers' Knowledge Determines Outcomes

In 1995, Raymond Chiao, a Hong Cong native and quantum physicist then teaching at the University of California at Berkeley, published a paper about a series of experiments. The paper, reported upon in a July 1995 issue of *Newsweek* magazine, said that what researchers knew or did not know about certain aspects of each experiment had a predictable determination on their outcomes. In other words, what was in the researchers' minds—i.e. thought—apparently determined the result. In the Newsweek article reporting on this, Nobel Prize winning physicist Richard Feynman was quoted as having said this is the "central mystery" of quantum mechanics, that something as intangible as knowledge—in this case, which slit a photon went through—changes something as concrete as a pattern on a screen.

In 2001, F. Holmes Atwater published the book already discussed detailing how in 1979 he set up and managed—until his retirement from the Army in 1988—a remote viewing unit of U. S. Army intelligence.

Prayer Adds Fuel to the Life Force

Also in 2001, a study published in the September issue of the Journal of Reproductive Medicine showed that prayer was able to double the success rate of in vitro fertilization procedures that lead to pregnancy. The findings revealed that a group of women who had people praying for them had a 50 percent pregnancy rate compared to a 26 percent rate in the group of women who did not have anyone praying for them. In the study—led by Rogerio Lobo, chairman of obstetrics and gynecology at Columbia University's College of Physicians & Surgeons—none of the women undergoing the IVF procedures knew about the prayers on their behalf. Nor did their doctors. In fact, the 199 women were in Cha General Hospital in Seoul, Korea, thousands of miles from those praying for them in the U.S., Canada and Australia. This collaborates with other studies and quantum physics theory that distance is not a factor at the subatomic level of mind.

Research Tells How Best to Pray

An organization exists that has as its purpose the study of what prayer techniques produce the best results. It's called Spindrift* and was founded by Christian Science practitioners who have been at this since 1975.

The first question Spindrift researchers sought to answer is, does prayer work? The answer, as we already know, is yes. In one test, rye seeds were split into groupings of equal numbers and placed in a shallow container on a soil-like substance called vermiculite. (For city dwellers, this is commonly used by gardeners.) A string was drawn across the middle to indicate that the seeds were divided into side A and side B. Side A was prayed for. Side B was not. A statistically greater number of rye shoots emerged from side A than from side B.

Variations of this experiment were devised and conducted, but not until this one was repeated by many different Christian Science prayer practitioners all of whom got consistent results.

Next, salt was added to the water supply. Different batches of rye seeds received doses of salt ranging from one teaspoon per eight cups of water to four teaspoons per eight cups. Doses were stepped up in increments of one-half teaspoon per batch.

A total of 2.3 percent more seeds sprouted on the prayed-for side of the first batch—one teaspoon per half-gallon of water—than on the not-prayed-for side—800 "prayed-for" seeds sprouted out of 2,000, versus 778 sprouts out of 2000 in the not-prayed-for side. As the dosage of salt was increased, the total number of seeds sprouting decreased, but the proportion of seeds that sprouted on the prayed-for sides increased, compared to the not-prayed-for sides, as the amount of the salt—stress—increased. In the 1.5 teaspoon batch, the increase was 3.3 percent. In the 2.0 teaspoon batch, 13.8 percent. In the 2.5 batch, 16.5 percent. In the 3.0, 30.8 percent. Five times as many prayed-for seeds in the 3.5 batch sprouted—although the total number which sprouted was small as can be seen from the chart below. Finally, no seeds sprouted in the 4.0 teaspoon per eight cup batch.

What this says is what people lying in a ditch with bombs going off around them have always known: the more dire the situation, the more helpful prayer will be. Up to a point. There comes a time when things are so bad nothing helps.

Studies similar to this have been and are being carried out by a consortium of scientists put together by Lynne McTaggart, author of the book published in 2002, *THE FIELD: The Quest for the Secret Force of the Universe*, and her 2008 release, *The INTENTION EXPERIMENT: Using Your Thoughts to Change Your Life* and the World. When she was on my show in early 2008, she described some of these experiments and the terrific success she and her colleagues have had. She said several of these studies were already being prepared for publication.

Mind Is Shown to Create Matter

In 2007, Stephen E. Braude published the book already discussed, *The Gold Leaf Lady and Other Parapsychological Investigations*. The book tells the story of Katie, a woman who demonstrates mind can produce matter—in this case brass: 80% copper and 20% zinc with its huge implications for quantum physics and he origins of the physical universe.

Mediums Relate Information about the Dead

Also in 2008, Julie Beischel, Ph.D., whose work was covered in Chapter Four, published a paper in *The Journal of Parapsychology* in which she concluded, " . . . certain mediums can report accurate and specific information about the deceased loved ones (termed discarnates) of living people (termed sitters) even without any prior knowledge about the sitters or the discarnates and in the complete absence of any sensory sitter feedback. Moreover, the information reported by these mediums cannot be explained as a result of fraud or 'cold reading' (a set of techniques in which visual and auditory cues from the sitter are used to fabricate 'accurate' readings) on the part of the mediums or rater bias on the part of the sitters."

This brings us to the present. I'd say it's about time for us to connect the dots. We will do so in the next chapter.

Chapter Thirteen
A New Worldview

We live in a world of information overload. So much comes at us every day it's impossible to take it all in. This may be one reason the water building up behind the dam has not yet broken through. Maybe so much information has numbed our minds, or put us all to sleep.

Nevertheless, the time has come to acknowledge we are not comparable to machines—as the nineteenth-twentieth century paradigm still holding sway would have us believe. We are not assemblies of parts that somehow evolved out of the muck and developed a computer-like organ called the brain that miraculously creates awareness inside our skulls. When the brain dies, the lights do not go out. We simply leave the old worn out vehicle behind and go on to other things.

The lights do not go out because the brain and the body are simply means to an end. The brain-body combination is a way for spirit—the life force, a spark of the godhead—to enter into physical reality. Perhaps we come here one time. Perhaps we come here hundreds or even thousands of times. Perhaps physical reality is like a great big amusement park—a diversion. Perhaps it is a school. I think it's both, and we come here to learn. What are we here to learn? Many things. But compassion may top the list. In the spirit realm, there are no starving people. There is no need to come up with rent money. There is no physical pain.

A Plausible View of the Afterlife

One view of the afterlife that I find plausible is that of the eighteen-century philosopher, scientist, and theologian, Emanuel Swedenborg (1688-1772). I learned about him and his teachings fairly recently from YouTube videos produced by the Swedenborg Foundation called, "Off the Left Eye."

Swedenborg claimed to have had a spiritual awakening at age 53 that allowed him to travel back and forth between the spiritual dimensions and the physical world. According to him, seven levels of the spiritual world exist, and we end up in the one that best suits us in terms of how evolved we are spiritually. In other words, we go to a place in the afterlife where we live, work, and play with others who are like us. So, what does that mean? What would land us on the top level?

As you know, according to Jesus, the Great Commandment is to love God with all your heart and all your soul and all your mind and your neighbor as yourself (see Matthew 22:36-40). Those who actually do that, not because they have been coerced to but because they want to, get to live in the highest level of heaven where everyone loves everyone else. As Swedenborg is reported to have said, "Love consists in desiring to give what is our own to another and feeling his delight as our own." Imagine what a great place that would be.

The levels below the highest are inhabited by those at progressively lower levels of spiritual evolution all the way down to hell. The inhabitants there hate others and want to do them harm.

So, according to Swedenborg, no one is sent to heaven or to hell. We simply go to a place in the afterlife that suits who we are and what we have become. If this true, we make our own heaven or hell, and that makes sense to me since it goes along with the idea that Earth is a school.

Whether or not you believe what Swedenborg taught, no matter what the reason or reasons we come here may be, the physical realm is not our home. Spirit is our home. This time in history is the right time for us to realize who we are and what we are doing here because many of us have lost our way. We've forgotten who we are. We have forgotten we are eternal, and that we are either evolving or devolving. We are sparks of the Divine. Getting more material stuff we will someday have to leave behind will not help us grow.

A New Worldview

In the past, a single discovery could create a new worldview—that the earth was round, or that the sun was the center of the solar system. Then Newton's laws followed by the Origin of Species did the trick. It seems to me so many discoveries have occurred since then that more than enough are on the table to create a new one.

What's holding us back? Those with a vested interest in maintaining the status quo. People who do not want to look stupid. Ignorance on the part of people too caught up in the information overload to see the forest for the trees. People with dogmatic religious beliefs. The truth is, a new worldview is already held in part by many, and in full by a small percentage of the population in the West today.

Ironically, the new world view is not fundamentally different from that which existed before self awareness caused humans to feel separated from the rest of nature. It is that mind—the intelligent medium of thought postulated by Thomas Troward—is the ground of being of all that is, and that we and everything in the universe are not only connected to it and to each other, we are each aspects of it. We are at one with nature, part of one mind. In our new understanding that the Divine animates us all, we have come full circle, yet we have arrived on higher ground in terms of our depth of our understanding.

Aspects and Implications of the New Worldview

The new worldview—that we are aspects of one mind—has a number of implications. It can accommodate both science and religion and bring the two together—although each will need to make adjustments to eliminate what will now be seen as aberrant dogma.

Both Thomas Troward and Scott Peck were correct. The ground of being is the life force, the medium of thought that pushes in the direction of growth and evolution—producing the phenomenon Peck called grace. The realization it exists solves the problem inherent in Darwin's theory of evolution—the lack of a counterbalance to the Law of Entropy.

Rupert Sheldrake is right. Sub fields exist within this field. Lovelock was correct—the earth, Gaia, has a field. Each species has a field. Each person has a field we call a soul. Sub fields are individual and yet at one with the whole just as television transmissions represent a single bandwidth and separate channels simultaneously.

The life force, Tao, or God does not play favorites. As Jesus said, "[God] causes his sun to rise on the evil and the good and sends rain on the righteous and unrighteous." (Matthew 5:45)

The field of mind supports and fosters life and harmony of body, mind and spirit. Prayer—some prefer the word "intention"—can add energy to this. Studies that show more and higher-quality prayer or intention will bring greater results.

How to Make Life Work and Purposeful

Because our minds are objective, we have the power of choice or "free will." This gives us the ability to attune our thoughts and actions with the direction of the life force—toward growth, evolution, and harmony. It gives us the power to recognize the compassionate self within. It gives us the power to go within and commune with the Universal Mind, the Tao, or the Holy Spirit—whatever name you may wish to give the ground of being within.

By aligning ourselves and subjugating our wills to the Universal Mind, we "go with the flow" and life works better for us. When we push against the force and try to counteract or contain it, we experience difficulties.

Synchronicities Are Real

The universal mind matches things up that may benefit from being matched up—called synchronicity—in its push toward growth and evolution. Life, health and harmony within an organism are supported perforce. In all matters, the outcome that will produce the maximum amount of evolution receives top priority. The Universal Mind will make events work in such a way that even the most horrible tragedy will produce the maximum good possible. This may be the meaning behind the Apostle Paul's words in Romans 8:28, "And we know that in all things God works for the good of those who love him." That they love him means they are striving to evolve in order to become more like him. Let's face it, difficulties often force us to evolve and to become better people as a result.

Our Views and Attitudes Create Our Experiences

God is within us. Therefore, the personality of the God our objective mind assumes exists will be the personality of the God we come to know because the subjective mind within plays back what we impress upon it. If we assume a loving and forgiving father God, as Jesus said to do, this will be our God. If someone assumes a loving mother God, instead, this will be that person's experience.

If one believes in an unforgiving, wrathful and capricious God, this will be the God that person has to deal with.

If a person does not believe in God at all, but thinks everything happens arbitrarily and by chance, this will be that person's experience.

If a person believes that God will punish him for his transgressions, that person will be punished. Outside circumstances combined with beliefs become a person's reality. To change your reality, change your beliefs.

The same is true in matters of health. If a person believes the body is subject to all sorts of influences beyond his control, and that this, that, or another symptom shows that such and such an uncontrollable influence is at work on him, then the belief will impress itself on the subjective mind, the subjective mind will accept it without question and proceed to fashion bodily conditions in accordance with the belief. Once someone fully grasps this, he or she will see it is just as easy to externalize healthy conditions as it is the contrary.

You Are Eternal, We All Are Eternal

What else?

Your current incarnation may be one of a long line than dates to the first life on earth, or some other planet. Your physical body is a projection of your morphogenetic field in combination with those of your parents, their genes, and the morphogenetic field of the species. In this lifetime you are a composite of your soul, which is eternal and timeless, the genes and morphogenetic field of the family you were born into, and the environment in which you grew up. The you of this life will eventually be incorporated into your soul as you evolve throughout eternity.

When we die, our souls return to spirit—the mental realm. We may be members of a group who work together. We may be guides to one another. We may incarnate together often—as part of a group of souls that cooperate to help one another advance.

All creation is one connected whole, with no separate pieces. We are the whole, and the whole is us. What happens here influences what happens there, even if it is halfway across the galaxy. Energy takes time to travel, but information is transmitted instantaneously because only one mind exists.

Cultivate Your Garden

Although I don't th ink it's always the case, each lifetime on Earth usually has a particular purpose. It may be to learn a lesson. It may be to help others in some way. Some have missions they agreed to before an incarnation. When this is the case, the circumstances of one's life support the accomplishment of that mission.

In my opinion, there is no greater joy in life than doing what you are here to do. Getting to that point may be difficult, but a person will get there if he or she listens and perseveres. Eventually, grace will kick in. After a while, a person following an innate calling will begin to sense unseen guiding hands, and the way will become less difficult. The trials won't be as hard to bear. There will be blind alleys, of course. There will be disappointments. There will be tough lessons to learn, but gradually that person will come to a gut level understanding of what his or her existence as a human being is about and the purpose of this particular life on earth. That person will come to know what he or she is doing and see outcomes materializing before the destination is reached.

When a person arrives at this point, that person will realize he or she has come to power, spiritual power, and with this realization will come joy. Imagine the buoyant feeling. Whether it's mastery of a sport such as golf or tennis, mastery of the card game of bridge, a musical instrument or a foreign language, the arrival at the state of really knowing what you are doing always brings joy.

Now that you have grasped the new worldview, that's what I wish for you. Mastery at what you came here to do. It makes sense to pursue it, don't you agree?

May the riches of the universe—which are in fact non-material—flow effortlessly to you because you are working with the universe, rather than rowing against the tide.

Life After Death Book II:

Heaven, Hell, & You

"God is at home, it's we who have gone out for a walk."

— Meister Eckhart (1260-1328)

Preface

I was raised by secular humanists, and like most in my generation, was taught by them in school and college. It's no wonder I bought into nineteenth and twentieth century scientific dogma that continues to maintain the material world—what you can see, touch, or measure—is all there is. Like many who still have the blinders on, I was convinced of that until the night I looked down at my body from the ceiling of my bedroom and was startled to see it lying on the bed, unconscious. I have been searching for answers about the true nature of reality ever since I had that out-of-body experience at the age of 27.

That, as of this writing, was more than four decades ago. During the intervening years I have devoured an enormous amount of material written by or about a large number of people, including Raymond Moody, Scott Peck, Alan Watts, Edgar Cayce, Jesus Christ, Stephen Braude, Rupert Sheldrake, Joseph Campbell, Emanual Swedenborg, Ian Stevenson, Eckhart Tolle, Gary Zukav, J.B. Rhine, Jim B. Tucker, Siddhārtha Gautama, Julie Beischel, Thomas Campbell, Bruce Greyson, Michael Newton, and many others.

In addition, I spent two years reading books and interviewing the authors of those books, who were parapsychologists, medical doctors, psychologists, psychiatrists, quantum physicists, and researchers into the true nature of reality for a radio show I produced and hosted called *The Truth about*

Life. One result is that I wrote a book that gleaned and boiled down the salient facts from the above called, *Life After Death, Powerful Evidence You Will Never Die.* If you have read that book, you know it lays out indisputable evidence that the brain does not create consciousness, but rather, the brain is a receiver comparable to a cell phone or radio that connects and integrates our consciousness with our bodies. To make a long story short, the upshot is that your consciousness will continue to exist after the body you currently are encased within draws its last breath.

This is intended as "Part Two" of that book.

Why a Part Two? Because, even though I described several near death experiences and what they are like, I spent only a page or so speculating about the long-range nature of the afterlife, such as in what environment a person is likely to end up, and I wrote nothing at all about hell, and whether it exists. The reason I didn't wasn't because I do not have a firm idea or a mental concept of the afterlife. The reason was that I wanted that initial book to be based solidly on facts and felt it important to omit as much speculation as possible in order to make an airtight case our consciousness can and will continue after death of the body.

When it comes to the nature of afterlife, however, particularly concerning what to expect after one has been on the other side for a while, not every source agrees. For example, the picture one gets from reading *Proof of Heaven* by Dr. Eben

Alexander is very different from what one takes away from Dr. Michael Newton's *Destiny of Souls,* or *Journey of Souls.* My reading of Dr. Alexander's book indicated to me a heaven that resembles a magnificent, dreamlike, sort of natural wilderness; whereas Dr. Newton's depiction of the afterlife (or more accurately, "life between lives") is structured, has classical-style buildings, including an enormous library that houses the Akashic Records, and it is populated by souls grouped together according to their level of development in what might be viewed as extended families, or tribes.

I have come to the conclusion differences are to be expected since heaven is a mental experience. As Jesus said in Luke 17:21, "The Kingdom of Heaven is within you."

The truth is that everything is a mental experience. Ask any trial lawyer. Different people typically will describe the same event quite differently, even under oath. Moreover, it appears that mind, or consciousness, is the ground of being of all reality, which adds credence to the claim we create our own reality, perhaps especially when it comes to the afterlife. In my book, *Amazing Truth,* I presented the findings of quantum physics experiments that any fair-minded person would have to agree is powerful evidence of that physical reality is a projection or creation of the Universal Mind. Your consciousness, and that ground-of-being Universal Mind consciousness, are one and the same. All of us arose from it and remain part of it. I will go into more detail shortly, as well as the implications, but let me first explain how I have arrived at my depiction of heaven and hell and what you can expect to encounter when the time comes for you, your consciousness, to leave your physical body behind.

I have taken into consideration everything I have read or heard from those who claim to know something about nonphysical reality, and in order to separate the wheat from the chaff have jettisoned what does not sync in some way with what others have written, or mesh with it in a way that helps create a coherent picture. I have formed what remains into a portrait of the afterlife wherein the details form an overall picture that hangs together as a total package. I feel justified in doing so because my personality type, according to the Myers-Briggs personality approach, is one that has an affinity for building theoretical models, which means I instantly spot contradictions and see how something over there has an impact on something over here. You see, I am one of less than two percent of the population, an INTJ, meaning I'm introspective, prefer intuition, rely on rational thought rather than feelings when considering veracity, and I'm constantly judging what I encounter, rather than passively perceiving it. One way this manifests is that what makes sense to me is much more important than who said it.

Some people don't like having me around because they have the feeling I see through them, like the little boy who shouted, "The king has no clothes!" while everyone else was thinking, "The king must have clothes. After all, he's the king. It must be me who just can't see them."

Not so for an INTJ. Read on and the portrait will unfold.

Chapter One

How We Got Here

God is love. You may consider that a cliché, but I believe it's true. God is love and three things more: He is the ground of being of all that is. He is infinite consciousness, and He is infinite wisdom.

Before I go further, let me say, if my use of the male pronoun bothers you, I apologize. I do not want to suggest that God is an old man with a long white beard, sitting on a cloud. That really is a cliché. But I'm not going to call God, "It," and the use of "She" would be limiting as well. God is neither male nor female; He is both. A good pronoun for God simply does not exist, so please forgive me for using, "Him."

On top of being the ground of being and infinite consciousness, love and wisdom, we humans are God's offspring. I am certain of that for a number of reasons, the most prominent of which is that love cannot exist by itself. Just as it takes two to tango, at least two individuals are required for love to exist: A lover and someone to love. This leads directly to the reason God created us. He did so to have offspring to love, and so He created us. It follows that He wants us to love Him back.

The next point I want to make is that God's love is not ordinary love. It's not like the puppy love your high school sweetheart had for you right before he or she dumped you and went with someone else to the junior-senior prom. So let's consider the ramifications of "God is love."

Here's what William Shakespeare said about love (Sonnet 116):

Let me not to the marriage of true minds
Admit impediments. Love is not love
Which alters when it alteration finds,
Or bends with the remover to remove.
O no! it is an ever-fixed mark
That looks on tempests and is never shaken;
It is the star to every wand'ring bark,
Whose worth's unknown, although his height be taken.
Love's not Time's fool, though rosy lips and cheeks
Within his bending sickle's compass come;
Love alters not with his brief hours and weeks,
But bears it out even to the edge of doom.
If this be error and upon me prov'd,
I never writ, nor no man ever lov'd.

Apparently, Shakespeare thought true love is more powerful than a tempest, perfectly steadfast, and as permanent as the Rock of Gibraltar—maybe more so.

Life After Death

Here's what the Apostle Paul had to say about love (1st Corinthians 13:4-8, NIV, 1984 ed.):

4 Love is patient, love is kind. It does not envy, it does not boast, it is not proud. 5 It is not rude, it is not self-seeking, it is not easily angered, it keeps no record of wrongs. 6 Love does not delight in evil but rejoices with the truth. 7 It always protects, always trusts, always hopes, always perseveres. 8 Love never fails. But where there are prophecies, they will cease; where there are tongues, they will be stilled; where there is knowledge, it will pass away.

Pretty strong stuff, don't you agree?

According to statements that have been a basic part of western civilization for 500 and 2000 years respectively, true love is nothing to sneeze at. And God's love has to be prefect, so you can multiply what Paul and Shakespeare said by an almost infinite factor. This is important because it has powerful implications concerning the nature of heaven and hell and how God deals with us, His children.

To begin to put this into perspective, let me ask you, do you have children? Do you love them? Of course you do. Do you forgive them when they make mistakes? I'll bet you do. When you got tough with them as children or teenagers, was it because you wanted to punish them, or was it because you wanted what was best for them in the long run?

You wanted them to grow up to be good, happy, and successful people, right?

Of course you did.

Well, God is your father and your mother. He-She-It wants what's best for you, which means He-She-It wants you to learn and grow, and more than anything, He-She-It wants you to love Him-Her-It back. That's why you were created, and ultimately, why the physical dimension was created.

Why Was Physical Reality Created?

Some people think souls existed before the physical universe came into being. Others think God used the physical universe as a vehicle to create us. The former think we are like sparks from the main fire that is God, sparks that existed for eons in nonphysical reality that eventually entered physical reality on a kind of adventure. We sparks tried out different kinds of bodies, which is how the myths of part human, part animal creatures such as satyrs, the sphinx, werewolves, and so forth came to be. Eventually human souls ended up choosing the ape-like, humanoid form we now inhabit, but during the meantime, we forgot how we got here and now are stuck on the wheel of life. Buddhists, Hindus and others who accept reincarnation as fact are looking for a way to get off the wheel so they can stay in nonphysical reality ("heaven") where existence is not so difficult. You agree, don't you, that life is difficult? You bet it is.

Another school of thought, and the one I buy into, is that God created physical reality, perhaps via a Big Bang, so He could "breathe" his spirit into matter and thereby create life and consciousness that functioned as though it were separate from Him and eventually would come to believe it actually was separate. As stated above, He wanted offspring to love, and physical reality was a way to create offspring with free will who were capable of loving Him and voluntarily becoming His companions. After all, no one I know would prefer a lover or companion who was forced to play that role.

Let me interject, parenthetically, that the gaping flaw in the nineteenth and twentieth century scientific materialist worldview that many still accept today is that no answer exists for what came before or caused the Big Bang. In my book about continuation of consciousness after death of the body, I included a quotation from British biochemist Rupert Sheldrake that calls attention to how ridiculous this flaw makes materialists look:

"[Scientific Materialists say] give us one free miracle and we'll explain the rest.' And the one free miracle is the appearance of all the matter and energy of the universe, and all the laws that govern it, from nothing in a single instant."

What existed before the Big Bang? Consciousness. What existed before consciousness? There was no "before." Consciousness always existed. It is eternal and as such has no beginning or end. Think about it. "Before" and "After" are functions of time, and according to quantum mechanics, time is a phenomenon of physical reality. Before physical reality existed, there was no time—no beginning, no end—simply eternity. Just ask a quantum physicist or a metaphysician about time if you have doubts about that.

How God Created Humans

We humans, and everything else in the universe evolved out of the organizing consciousness that is God. Following the Big Bang, He created RNA followed by DNA and then one-celled animals, which eventually led to an almost infinite number of variations of living things. Those most suited to the environment survived. These living things reproduced by the millions, each offspring slightly different from its siblings. Again, those that adapted to the environment survived and reproduced. And on and on. All of living things were infused with His consciousness, as they are today.

As evolution progressed, the consciousness of many living organisms became more an more organized, or to use another word, "intelligent." This intelligence impressed itself upon the organizing intelligence of spirit, and the organizing intelligence of spirit went to work to create ever more sophisticated and evolved adaptations.

Consider this: if matter is all that is as today's scientific dogma maintains, consciousness could not and would not have existed until evolution produced a brain. Yet plants possess consciousness. In my yard, they grow toward the sun, so they must have some level of consciousness about where the sun is. But according to the materialist worldview, consciousness is the result of electrons jumping across synapses in the brain—a sort of rainbow-type illusion, which materialists believe came about due to an incredible number of accidents, something like thousands of monkeys banging away on typewriters until one produced *War and Peace* from start to finish with no typos. Mathematicians tell us the odds of that are one in infinity, which is another way of saying it's not impossible. Yet scientific materialist theory ignores this and two more important facts: 1) the brain does not create consciousness, i.e., it is a receiver of consciousness (see my previous book for conclusive evidence), and 2) throughout the eons of evolution, needs have preceded the organs through which they are fulfilled—eyes, ears, taste buds, hearts, kidneys, lungs, and so forth. Charles Darwin himself said it was absurd to think natural selection produced something as complicated as eyes. It seems pretty clear instead that each new organ developed in response to a need, which in the case of eyes was to see, so why would the brain be an exception? The need for which the brain was created was to capture and organize something that has always existed: consciousness.

The result of the process of evolution I have just briefly touched on has been ever-increasing levels of intelligence displayed by ever-more complex and evolved life forms. This is how we came to be and how God created entities that could be bona fide companions. As creatures evolve and their brains are more sophisticated, they are more and more intelligent, until eventually they are self-aware. Flowers, plants, and earthworms possess only subjective or subconscious minds, their own small portions of underlying, ground-of-being, organizing intelligence. Their "minds" are subjective because they cannot think about themselves. They can only react in a programmed way to the input or stimuli they receive. Highly evolved mammals and to a greater extent, humans, have both a subjective mind and an objective mind. Their subjective minds keep them breathing and their bodies functioning while their objective minds think about and analyze situations. They can even think about themselves and wonder why they are here in physical reality.

Unlike the subjective mind, an objective mind can worry and be afraid. This is both a blessing and a curse. It is a blessing in that we can plan ahead in order to avoid trouble and thereby eliminate the uncomfortable sensation of worry. It is a curse because worry is a kind of fear, and fear is a kind of belief charged with emotion. Since it does not analyze or judge, the subjective mind works to bring about what the objective mind believes. That, however, is something to explore in a different book, so let me refrain from wandering off point and say that the allegory in Genesis about Adam and Eve in the Garden of Eden is about the epoch in evolution when we humans evolved to the point we developed objective minds and thereby became self-aware. This resulted in free will in that we no longer had to follow our instincts, or what might be referred to as the "still small voice within." Let's look at that part of the story, which occurs in Chapter Three, verses 1-7 (NIV, 1984 ed.):

Now the serpent was more crafty than any of the wild animals the Lord God had made. He said to the woman, "Did God really say, 'You must not eat from any tree in the garden'?"

The woman said to the serpent, "We may eat fruit from the trees in the garden, but God did say, 'You must not eat fruit from the tree that is in the middle of the garden, and you must not touch it, or you will die.'"

"You will not surely die," the serpent said to the woman. "For God knows that when you eat of it your eyes will be opened, and you will be like God, knowing good and evil."

When the woman saw that the fruit of the tree was good for food and pleasing to the eye, and also desirable for gaining wisdom, she took some and ate it. She also gave some to her husband, who was with her, and he ate it.

Then the eyes of both of them were opened....

Up to this point in evolution, Adam and Eve (we humans) had lived an idyllic life, communing with God and enjoying

His creation. We were like characters in the Disney movie, *The Lion King*, with no worries, singing the song, "Hakuna Matata." In other words, we were creatures living in a habitat to which we were perfectly adapted. What caused us to separate from that idyllic life was our newly developed ego, which I believe is what the crafty serpent represents. Eve's ego led her down a path by telling her she would not die if she ate the fruit. It used a motivation we humans have in spades, especially primitive humans, which is to be like God. To be like God is to possess power to the highest degree. Just think how many humans throughout recorded history have wanted that, and have strived to grasp it. That same motivation hooked Eve, intrigued her, and caused her to move ahead.

The text goes on to say that Eve then recognized the fruit was pleasing to the eye. In other words, it was desirable because of how it looked, aesthetically. This fueled a desire in her to acquire the fruit, just as people today are motivated to acquire wealth, and thereby, the many beautiful possessions money can buy.

A third motivation was that the fruit was desirable for gaining wisdom. Prestige comes from being knowledgeable, just as it does from being wealthy. Power, wealth, and prestige are basic human motivators, and that's what we humans wanted once we developed egos.

Thus entities (humans) were produced that considered themselves separate from God, entities He could love that had the ability to freely choose to love Him back, which is what He intended from the start. The point of the story, of course, is that we humans chose to go our separate way. But that isn't the end of the story. The rest of it is how God has arranged things, and continues arranging them, in an effort to get us to choose to return to Him.

We're on a Hero's Journey

Have you ever considered why we humans often become so enthralled by stories? The really good ones usually contain the same elements. Myths of every culture recount the same tale repeatedly, each in its own cultural guise. A hero or heroine is either compelled or "called" to leave the safety and security of home and venture into the unknown where real or metaphorical dragons and demons must be faced and overcome. *The Wizard of Oz* is a prototypical example. A cave (the witch's castle) must be entered and the broom brought back to the wizard. Supported by unseen or supernatural powers, the hero who pushes forward invariably will succeed, later to return home (the farm in Kansas) more highly evolved than when he or she left and in possession of the elixir, i.e., a new, higher level of understanding. ("There's no place like home.")

This is what life in the physical dimension is about. Each of us, and all of us, are on a hero's journey. We leave the comfort of home—the non-physical world of spirit —and we come into the physical world via our mother's womb to face inevitable difficulties and struggles, to slay proverbial demons and dragons, and ultimately to return home wiser and more highly evolved than when we left.

Our sojourns to Earth are hero's adventures, but they are not the only ones we take. We usually experience a number of smaller adventures during each lifetime. Our society ignores this phenomenon, even though the call comes whenever the time is at hand for an individual to move to a higher plane of understanding. The denial of such a basic component of life can lead to tragedy in that dire consequences typically result from a refusal to accept the call. Warnings of this can be found in myths throughout the ages. Refusal converts what otherwise would be positive and constructive into negative form. The would-be hero loses the power of action and becomes instead a victim bound by boredom, hard work, or even imprisonment.

Many myths relate this same tale; I'll give you a couple of cases in point. King Minos, for example, refused the call to sacrifice the bull, which would have signified his submission to the Divine. Of course, he didn't know that this would have resulted in his elevation to a higher state. So instead, like a modern day business executive or professional, he became trapped by conventional thinking and attempted to overcome the situation through hard work and determination. Indeed, he was able to build a palace for himself, just as many executives and professionals today build their mansions in the suburbs. But it turned out to be a wasteland, a house of death, a labyrinth in which to hide, and thus escape from the horrible Minotaur.

And look at what happened to Daphne, the beautiful maiden pursued by the handsome Greek god, Apollo. He wished only to be her lover, and called to her, "I who pursue you am no enemy. You know not from whom you flee. It is only for this reason that you run."

All Daphne had to do was submit, to accept the call, and beautiful and bountiful love would have been hers. She, too, would have had a relationship with the Divine. But as you probably know, she did not submit. She kept running, and as a result turned into a laurel tree, and that was the end of her.

Now let me relate one more. It is the same as the two above, and conveys the same warning. This time it comes from Jesus, and it applies directly to you and me. It can be found in all three synoptic gospels. This account is from Mark 10:17-23, the New International Version (NIV) translation:

> *As Jesus started on his way, a man ran up to him and fell on his knees before him. "Good teacher," he asked, "what must I do to inherit Eternal Life?"*
>
> *"Why do you call me good?" Jesus answered. "No one is good—except God alone. You know the commandments: 'Do not murder, do not commit adultery, do not steal, do not give false testimony, do not defraud, honor your father and mother.'"*

"Teacher," he declared, "all these I have kept since I was a boy."

Jesus looked at him and loved him. "One thing you lack," he said. "Go, sell everything you have and give to the poor, and you will have treasure in heaven. Then come, follow me."

At this the man's face fell. He went away sad, because he had great wealth.

Jesus looked around and said to his disciples, "How hard it is for the rich to enter the Kingdom of God!"

The disciples were amazed at his words. But Jesus said again, "Children, how hard it is to enter the Kingdom of God! It is easier for a camel to go through the eye of a needle than for a rich man to enter the Kingdom of God."

Well, there you are. If ever a person received the call to adventure, it was this rich young man. As with Minos and Daphne, the promise is that he will eventually experience the ecstasy of a relationship with the Divine. But first, as was the case with those two before him, he would have to give up his earthly treasure. This is the ultimate call to adventure, and the one we are all ultimately are required to undertake. Hopefully, this will become clear to you by the time you finish this book, and you will be ready to go for it, so stay tuned.

Chapter Two
Heaven Explored

Quite a bit is known about what to expect in the first half hour or so after death of the body because a large number of near death experiences (NDEs) have been reported upon over the last forty years. I covered much of this in *Life After Death, Powerful Evidence You Will Never Die,* so if you have read that book, please forgive the repetition. Rest assured, however, I have added to what I wrote in that book.

The first thing people experience upon death is that they are no longer contained within their bodies. A vivid example is what Pam Reynolds experienced when her body was drained of blood and shut down completely so that doctors could repair two ballooned arteries, one of which was located at the base of her brain near where the stem joined her spine.

The operation began at 7:15 a.m. on August 8, 1991, when anesthesia was administered. Both ear channels were occluded with molded ear speakers designed to monitor brain stem function. An electroencephalogram (EEG) was set up to monitor cortical brain waves. Flat lines displayed once her heart was stopped and the blood drained from her. That's when she heard a buzzing, an unpleasant sound reminiscent of a dentist's drill.

Here is what she recalled:

"I remember the top of my head tingling, and I just sort

of popped out of it. Then, I was looking down at my body. I knew it was my body, but for some reason I didn't care.

"My vantage point was that of sitting on the doctor's shoulder. He had an instrument in his hand that looked like an electric toothbrush. That puzzled me. I had assumed they would open the skull with a saw—I'd heard the term 'saw'—but what he was working with looked a lot more like a drill than a saw—sort of like my electric toothbrush—and there also was a case, like the one my father stored his socket wrenches in when I was a child—with little bits in it.

"I also heard people talking. I distinctly remember hearing a female voice say, 'We have a problem. The arteries are too small.'

"Someone said to try the other side.

"This [talking] seemed to come from somewhere down at the other end of the table and I wondered, 'What are they doing? This is brain surgery [not surgery on the legs].'

"I later found out they accessed the femoral arteries, which are in the groin area, in order to drain the blood from my body.

"I [soon] felt a presence, and I turned around to look at it. That's when I saw a tiny pinpoint of light.

"It [the light] started to pull me. There was a physical sensation like what you might have in your stomach when you drive fast over a hill. So I went toward the light, and as I came closer I began to discern different figures.

"I distinctly heard my grandmother call me. She had a

very distinct voice, and I immediately went to her. It felt great. And I saw an uncle who had passed away when he was only 39 years old. He had taught me a lot. He taught me to play my first guitar. I saw many people I knew and many I did not know."

Pam's experience was typical. Those who have crossed over and come back from the other side often have memories of vivid sensory imagery, and an extremely clear memory of what they experienced. They often describe what they experienced as seeming "more real" than their everyday life.

Often people report that time stopped or ceased to exist. The change in thinking phenomenon often includes a sudden revelation or change in understanding in which everything about universe and existence suddenly becomes crystal clear. There may also be a sense of the person's thoughts going much faster and being much clearer than usual. Typical emotions include an overwhelming sense of peace and wellbeing, a sense of cosmic unity and of being one with everything, a feeling of complete joy, and a sense of being loved unconditionally.

Sometimes people report seeing colors and hearing sounds that do not exist in this life, and a sense of extrasensory perception, i.e., of knowing things beyond the normal ability of the senses such as something happening at a remote location. Moreover, one can expect to be greeted by those from this life who have gone before, and perhaps by spirit guides or angelic beings who welcome new arrivals and help them transition from earthly life to existence in the spirit realm.

Often, those who have an NDE experience a life review—a panoramic memory in which the person's life unfolds before him or her in minute detail. I imagine this happens to everyone who dies and does not return. Spirit guides typically assist individuals who go through this and help them by providing guidance, perspective, and comfort. Sometimes a panel of what might be considered elders is present to assist in this regard.

Finally, with respect to NDEs, many survivors report they came to a border they could not cross, a point of no return, and had they gone past it, they would have bared from returning to life. Many also say they encountered a mystical or divine being, such as Jesus, in addition to other spirits, guides, and loved ones who had died previously. The spirits, relatives, and the being welcomed them into the afterlife, and in some cases, sent them back to life.

What about Hell?

Not everyone has such a rosy near death experience. Some say they went to hell, and that the life review was a horrid experience. A few years ago, I gave a sermon at a Unity Fellowship Church in Williamsburg, Virginia, during which I touched on the life review and its implications. After the service a man came up to me and told me about an NDE and life review a friend of his had recounted. I'll call the man's friend Ralph.

Life After Death

Apparently, before his NDE, Ralph had anger issues and a hair-trigger temper. Some time before Ralph's NDE, he had been driving along, minding his own business, when a car had pulled out in front of him, causing a fender-bender. Ralph became enraged, jumped out of his car, pulled the offending driver out of his, and beat him to a pulp. This beating left the offending driver permanently handicapped and unable to earn a living. Ralph was charged with assault and punished by the legal system, but that punishment was nothing compared to what he experience during his life review.

Not only did Ralph feel the hurt and sorrow of the man he'd injured, he also experienced the sorrow and misery of everyone who had been affected, and everyone who would be affected, including the man's children who were unable to attend college and had to go to work at early ages because of the family's reduced income. Ralph felt the hurt and sorrow experienced by the man's wife and other family members who were forced to care for the injured man and to work at menial jobs in order to put food on the table. The list of those whose sorrow Ralph experienced was long. It included the injured man's descendants who would be affected in future generations by the domino effect the beating Ralph gave would eventually cause. As you might suspect, Ralph was deeply affected by this, turned his life around, and became a different man as the result of his NDE and life review.

A similar story comes to mind, which I heard from a man interviewed for my radio show. He told me about a hell-like experience he had while clinically dead. This was not the same as a life review. The man said he had literally gone to hell because of the life he'd led up to that point as the member of a malicious gang. The experience affected him so deeply that he completely changed and became a Christian pastor.

Rather than relate the experience he described, however, I have extracted a passage from an Amazon.com review by a reader of one of my books that contains information about near death experiences. I think this conveys what my radio guest wanted to communicate. It appears to have been written by a nurse:

"While reading this book, I was reminded of a patient I had several years ago. She was in the final stages of death, and it was very early in the morning. She was screaming this horrid scream (one of those you just don't forget) and so I went in to sit with her. She had no family with her and I couldn't bear to let this woman breathe her last on her own. After sitting there for a few minutes, she asked me to uncover her feet, that they were really hot. A few minutes later, she asked me to uncover her legs. This went on for a while and soon she was drenched in sweat and writhing in pain. She told me to be a better person than she was because she was experiencing hell and it was something she hoped no one would ever have to experience. Before her final breaths, she was wrapped in ice-covered blankets to hopefully

make her transition somewhat more peaceful. This was the most horrid death that I've ever witnessed."

The International Association of Near-Death Studies estimates the incidence of distressing near death experiences ranges from 1% to 15% of all NDEs, which suggests the percentage of those who have a hell-like experience is low. I seriously doubt, however, that Adolph Hitler, Joseph Stalin, or Jeffrey Dahmer went to heaven.

Nevertheless, the pleasant near death experiences most people have, as well as those that are hell-like, may not be permanent. No one I know of has crossed the "un-crossable" border mentioned earlier and returned to tell the tale.

Why the First Taste of Heaven Likely Fades

The goal of life and evolution—the objective our many hero's journeys—is to reunite with God and to become His cherished companions, and unfortunately, many if not most of us are not ready for that. Edgar Cayce, the twentieth century's most documented psychic, gave more than 14,000 readings while in a self-induced trance. As revealed in the well-written and edifying book called *Many Mansions* by Dr. Gina Cerminara that's based on those readings, most of us incarnate many times before we evolve to the point that coming back for another go is no longer necessary. I don't know how many different individuals are represented in the 14,000 readings, but I have read that Cayce told only eight people this was their final incarnation on Earth. Nevertheless, there is a "life between lives" for those who eventually reincarnate. According to esoteric knowledge I've been privy to and studied, the average duration from one incarnation to the next is 140 years. Although it can be quite a lot longer, or much shorter, this suggests that on average if someone lives to age 70 on Earth, that person can expect to spend 70 years in the nonphysical reality before he or she returns to the physical plane via his or her new birth mother's womb.

In the next chapter we will explore what we might expect that sojourn in the nonphysical realm of spirit to be like.

Chapter Three

What Heaven Is Like

It seems to me the heaven most people have heard about or imagine is not a place many people would actually want to spend eternity, or even 70 years. For example, who would want to sit on a cloud all day, playing a harp? Who would want to spend eternity in a church pew, praising God or signing hymns? Such images of heaven are simplistic, but they are what a lot of people think, which prompted Mark Twain to quip, "Go to heaven for the climate. Hell for the company."

The truth is that heaven is much more and has much more to offer than we can possibly imagine while we are on this side of paradise. Most certainly it must be a vast and constantly expanding, limitless dimension of consciousness. Several sources indicate, for example, that there are different levels of heaven, and that many areas exist within those levels where people reside depending on where they are in terms of evolution, the culture or religion they are part of, and what they have become over the course of their lives. After all, "The Kingdom of Heaven is within you," meaning heaven is a mental place that we create based on our beliefs and attitudes. Therefore, heaven must be somewhat different for every individual. You probably would not feel comfortable or be happy in a heaven for Bushmen from the African savanna or members of the Korowai tribe of cannibals from Indonesian New Guinea. The heaven you will feel comfortable in is one in which others share your worldview and level of empathy, or lack there of for others. It is one where you will be able to live as you want and do as you wish, but let me say this. If it is not the top level heaven where everyone loves one another, serves one another and communes with God, you will likely have to return to earth in another incarnation in order to continue your personal evolution toward that top-level. My advice, therefore, is to begin now to follow your bliss by using your talents in the service of others. It's never too late to begin, and that is what will eventually get you to the top.

My experience after living a lifetime is that those who use their talents in the service of others are far more likely to feel happy, content, and fulfilled than those who do not. Accumulating money alone does not lead to fulfillment, or contentment, at least not for very long. Three things are required beyond a big bank account: a sense of peace, a lack of (or release from) guilt, and acceptance by others for who we are, rather than what we possess, or the position we happen to fill. Of course we must earn enough money, accumulate enough, or inherit enough to enable us to take care of our physical needs, such as food and shelter. But beyond that, the sense of helping others and being part of something larger than we are is what really matters. This is why Jesus was spot on when he replied upon being asked what the greatest commandment was:

> *"'Love the Lord your God with all your heart and with all your soul and with all your mind.' This is the first and greatest commandment. And the second is like it: 'Love your neighbor as yourself.'"* (Matthew 22:36-40, NIV)

Loving God means loving and serving what He has created. Loving your neighbor means serving your neighbors and wanting for them what you want for yourself. It seems to me those who actually do that, not because they have been coerced or forced into doing so but because they actually want to, are likely to ascend to the highest level of heaven where everyone loves and serves everyone else. These folks walk with God in the cool of the evening as Adam and Eve did before being cast out of the Garden, which means they have completed their hero's journeys and returned home to the Garden with elixir in hand. I picture them as angels that dart around helping humans avoid trouble, answering prayers, and comforting the forlorn, and as co-creators with God who are perhaps sent on missions to create, or to impart wisdom to, new or emerging worlds.

The levels below the highest are inhabited by those at progressively lower levels of spiritual evolution all the way down to hell. The inhabitants of the very bottom level hate others and want to do them harm.

By the way, I am as certain as I can be that no one is sent to heaven or cast into hell. Peter is not standing at the Pearly Gate, checking his book and giving new arrivals a thumbs up or a thumbs down. After your life review and a period of adjustment, you will cross that barrier and go to a place that suits the person you have become. It will be populated with people like you—no better and no worse. According to Michael Newton's books, those surrounding you will be your soul group and will consist of people you know well and have been evolving with for eons. They may in fact be, or have been, family members or friends and co-workers in this life as well as in others.

How God Keeps Us on Track

At the risk of becoming repetitious, let me repeat that heaven and hell are mental places and that means we build our own nest, or make our own bed so to speak, in the afterlife. Because we have free will, we can get ourselves way off course and end up in a place we don't want to be. God, however, has a way to keep us headed in the right direction if we will only pay attention. It's called Karma, and it encourages us to seek harmony.

When the Apostle Paul said, "A man reaps what he sows," (Galatians 6:7) he was talking about Karma, which is cause and effect. If throw a rock into a pond, you will disturb the harmony of the pond. You were the cause, and the effect was the splash. The ripples flow out, and they flow back, until harmony is restored. In the same way, disharmonious karmic actions go out into your reality and come back upon you until harmony is restored.

Edgar Cayce (1877-1945) dealt with the concept of Karma in detail. To fully understand it, you might want to read the book I mentioned earlier the full title of which is *Many Mansions: The Edgar Cayce Story on Reincarnation.* According to Cayce's psychic readings, Karma is not punishment. It is a learning tool. We humans will continue to meet situations similar to those that created the Karma until we start making the right choices. We are each like the character in the movie *Groundhog Day* who is forced to experience the same day over and over until he reacts to each situation with harmony and love, rather than with cynicism. Only then does he handle things correctly. Once the quality of his consciousness has evolved to a level that produces right action, he not only gets the girl, he is finally able to move on to February 3rd.

The universe and all energy function as a yin-yang balance, resulting in a tension between opposites. Yin is negative. Yang is positive. We all contain these dual aspects expressed as love and fear (which is a form of hate), harmony and chaos, good and evil. Tension is necessary for structures to exist, and we are energy structures. As such, we should not make the mistake of thinking that negative is always bad. A storage battery provides an analogy. One plate is charged positive, the next negative, the next positive, the next negative, and so on. Interaction between the plates generates the energy. The negative plate is not better or worse than the positive plate. Everything, us included, needs tension to exist.

Nevertheless, it is true most of us express our yin energy in undesirable ways such as excess hard work, gambling, dangerous activities such as drinking too much, driving too fast, or by arguing or fighting. Illness is an expression of yin energy. War is the ultimate expression. But yin energy can be expressed in different, non-destructive ways, such as positive challenges. Each of us must have a challenge to strive for and will self-destruct without one.

We all will benefit from understanding the importance of harmony and the ill effects of the lack of it. For example, that which you resist you draw to you, and in doing so will perpetuate its influence upon your life. If you are extremely resistant to your mother in law, for example, the result will be continual conflicts with her. If, however, you stop resisting by consciously releasing your feelings toward her and ignoring situations that come about that would otherwise draw you in, the problem you had with her will dissolve. It may not seem possible, but most disharmonious situations can be resolved with a change of viewpoint. Change your perspective and often you can eliminate the problem because you are no longer affected by it. Nothing has to change but your view of what's going on.

Here's something else to understand: "That which you resist, you become, if not in this lifetime, in a future incarnation." So, for example, if you resist or fear people of another race, next time you might incarnate as someone of that race. What better way to overcome a fear but to become what you fear?

My reason for going into this is that until you resolve your Karma and fully become the individual you have the potential to become, you will continue to incarnate. You alone decide what you most need to learn on your earthly sojourns. In each life you seek out other souls, some with shared histories, and always those with karmic issues matching your needs.

It's important to know that whenever you act with intension and create disharmony, you pile up karmic debt. Thoughts, emotions, and words are just as powerful at creating Karma as deeds are. The motives and desires behind what you think, feel, and do are what count. Disharmonious acts, thoughts, and so forth must be balanced in this life or in a future one unless you mitigate the Karma you have created by gaining the wisdom required to over come it.

Let me emphasize, however, that mechanically obeying the rules will not do you much good, at least not at first. It is, however, a way to begin. As you follow the rules and time goes by, you will begin to internalize the wisdom behind them. For this to happen, you must "fake it until you feel it." Eventually, the wisdom created will erase your karmic debt. By "wisdom," I mean a sense of knowing what is true and good by observing what works. Learn to love others, and you will mitigate your suffering.

Sadly, however, most of us seem to learn fastest through pain—through directly experiencing the consequences of our actions. Touch a hot stove, for example, and you won't do that again. Less obviously, if you greedily take from others instead of learning through wisdom and love that it's wrong, you will have to learn directly from experience how it feels to be violated in this way—either in this life, or in a future one. An alternative is to learn and follow the rules. Then, as you move toward a Karmic test, you will proceed with harmony, which will mitigate the impact of the event.

Here's an example. Let's say that in your last life you were married to a soul who is your mate today. In that previous life, you cruelly left your mate for another. Before you were born into this lifetime, you and your former mate agreed he or she would leave you under similar circumstances. This will allow you to balance your Karma and to directly experience the pain and sorrow of abandonment.

If through wisdom, however, you realize it is easier and less harmful for all involved for you to detach from the relationship with love, you will ease the pain of parting while also passing the test you set up for yourself.

Here is another example. Assume you have predestined a severe relationship test for September of your 29th year. In the meantime, you have learned to seek harmony by being positive, non judgmental, and without expectations in your relationships. As a result, you may only experience an argument with your mate on that fateful September day. If, however, you have not learned and instead operate with knee-jerk reactions, which without doubt will have intensified the disharmony in your relationship, you will likely experience a divorce.

Here's another: In your most recent past life you were so proud you were unwilling to accept assistance from others. Pride is a form of fear. As a result, in this life you have predestined an event that will cause you to be institutionalized for many years. On a soul level, you decided you needed to create circumstances that would force you to subdue your pride and allow others to give to you. But through wisdom, you have overridden your pride, opened your heart, and gladly accept assistance from others. Because of this, you will not have to be institutionalized. Wisdom has erased the Karma.

Okay, I can hear someone saying, "Does this mean I have to roll over and play dead? Become a patsy? Do I always have to give in to others?"

No. For example, you must never give in to abject evil. Adolph Hitler, Stalin, Kim Jong-un, the Iranian Mullahs, and the Islamic State are examples of evil personified that cannot be appeased. Evil is rebellion against God and the desire to be all-powerful as God is. As such, evil will view any attempt at compromise as weakness. This over-the-top form of evil is all about disharmony. Chaos is its stock and trade.

Fortunately, abject evil is rare. Usually, it is possible to find common ground with an adversary, and in doing so, to achieve harmony. Your objective should be to restore harmony, and this can often be done by looking for and finding a win-win solution. You may be surprised at how fast an agreement that resolves the issue can be reached.

The bottom line is that Karma can be experienced to the letter of the law, or it can be mitigated by mercy and grace. If you give others love, mercy and grace, you will receive the same in return.

It has been said that if you want friends, you must be a friend. If you want to be loved, you must love others. Such actions will greatly increase the quality of your life. Suffice it to say that things will begin to fall into place when you are in harmony with the universe. It's as though you are a magnet, drawing what you need to you. The greater your desire, the more you power you will give to the creative force of grace to assist you. Every Soul, living and discarnate, is connected at the level of the Infinite Mind. We are all one.

I picture the whole, Infinite Mind, Universal Consciousness or God, as "The Big Dreamer," and each individual soul, including yours and mind, as a character within the dream of God who each is having his or her own dream. The Big Dreamer sees the whole and is able to orchestrate it for the ultimate good of all. We are almost certain to have trials and tribulations along the way, but as long as our intentions are good and in line with the Great Commandment, things will work out for us in the end. God ultimately is in charge, and he wants what is best for you. He wants you to make it to the top.

Here's what Jesus' brother James had to say about this: "You do not have, because you do not ask God. When you ask, you do not receive, because you ask with wrong motives, that you may spend what you get on your pleasures." (James 4:2-3, NIV)

In other words, our motives need to be in line with God's goal, which is for us to become His companions. God is not in the business of satisfying our selfish whims. He wants something much more valuable. He wants us to evolve. He wants us to return to Him so that we can be His co-creators. Then we will truly live in heaven.

James also said, "Consider it pure joy, my brothers, whenever you face trials of many kinds, because you know that the testing of your faith develops perseverance. Perseverance must finish its work so that you may be mature and complete, not lacking anything." (James 1:2-4, NIV)

In other words, trials and hardships make us better people because we learn from them. In particular, we learn empathy and perseverance. That's why life on Earth is difficult. It's why bad things happen to good people, and also why every dark cloud has a silver lining. Things may be difficult now, but when you look back with the perspective time and distance give, you will realize you are a better person because of all that you went through and were able to endure.

Chapter Four
The Stages of Spiritual Growth

Several theories have been put forth concerning the evolution of souls, including one that describes the various stages one passes through as he or she grows spiritually. I came across one I believe is accurate in Scott Peck's book, *Further Along The Road Less Traveled.* As you read ahead, perhaps you'll see some of your co-workers, your boss—perhaps even your Uncle Charlie.

Stage One is the Chaotic/Antisocial. People at this level are unprincipled and antisocial. In effect, Stage One is a condition totally absent of spirituality. While they may pretend to love others, all of their relationships are self-serving and manipulative. Truly, they are looking out for number one. Being unprincipled, they have nothing to govern themselves except their own wills, which is why people in this stage are often found in trouble or difficulty, in jail, in hospitals, or whatever. It is possible for them to be self-disciplined from time to time and in the service of their ambition to rise to positions of prestige and power.

Some evangelistic preachers and politicians may fit into this category. I was once acquainted with someone I now recognize as a Stage One individual who headed a successful company. Under his direction the firm became one of the fastest growing in its field. The man was a brilliant speaker and strategist. He had a photographic memory. But he was totally without principles or anything close to what might be called a conscience. Even though he was married, he took pride in himself as a master of seduction of members of the opposite sex. Figuratively speaking, he left the landscape strewn with the bodies of his lovers and adversaries, and to my knowledge, he never felt an inkling of remorse. This man was extremely successful for a time and made millions before the age of forty. But in the end, his closest colleagues turned on him. They ejected him from the firm he'd helped to build, perhaps because they feared they too would someday become victims of his egocentric nature. This was the principle of cause and effect at work. What goes around indeed comes around—though one can never be sure how long it will sometimes take to come back around.

The Stage One person can have a difficult time of it if he ever happens to get in touch with himself and realizes the chaos within and the hurt he has caused others. It seems possible that such anguish may be the root cause of some unexplained suicides. A happier possibility is that the Stage One personality may suddenly and dramatically convert to Stage Two, which Peck has labeled the Formal/Institutional. Those at this place in evolution depend on an institution to keep them on the straight and narrow. This may be a prison, the military, or a rigidly organized corporation. For many in our society it is the Church.

Stage Two individuals tend to be attached to ritual and dogma and become very upset if someone challenges it or tries to institute change. We all know of those who take the Bible literally, who believe the world was created in six twenty-four hour days and that man was brought into being as a fully-evolved homo sapiens known as Adam. Rather than viewing the story as a myth about the ascent of man from a primate ruled by instinct into a human with free will, they believe that God literally banished the very first man—whose name was Adam—and the very first woman—whose name was Eve—from an actual idyllic spot known as the Garden of Eden.

Stage Two people think of God as an external being and almost always envision him as on a cloud looking down, making a list and checking it twice. More than likely they picture a man who looks remarkably like Michelangelo's depiction on the ceiling of the Sistine Chapel, and they ascribe to him the power and the will to make them extremely sorry for their transgressions. God is seen as a giant benevolent cop in the sky.

I want to state clearly, however, that many Christians, and no doubt followers of other religions, are by no means stuck in Stage Two. I personally know many who are well into Stage Four and even Stage Five. A characteristic of more advanced believers is an image of God as immanent in all of creation and a belief that at least some of what is presented in the Bible falls into the category of allegory.

Let's move on and consider the characteristics of Stage Three. It's not surprising that members of this group are likely to have been raised in a family headed by Stage Two parents (whether Christian, Buddhist, or Jewish) and as a result internalized their parents' religious and moral principles. By the time they reached adolescence, however, they were questioning the dogma. ("I looked at porn on the web and God didn't strike me blind. Who needs these silly myths and superstitions?") To the horror of their parents they eventually fell away from the Church and became doubters, or agnostics, or perhaps even atheists. This is the Skeptic/Individual stage. Its members are not religious, but neither are they antisocial. They are often deeply involved in social or ecological causes. Often they are scientists and almost always are scientific-minded. To my way of thinking, they comprise a plurality of the educated middle and upper middle class in America. They can be found in large numbers teaching our children and young adults in schools and universities. The media are chock full of them. They are reporters, columnists and commentators. Because they frequently rigidly adhere to mechanistic views of reality, and to secular humanist philosophy, they often strike Stage Two and Four/Five individuals as misguided. They are usually unwilling to consider the existence of anything they cannot see or touch. Many, however, do tend to be truth seekers, and if they seek truth deeply enough and widely enough and get enough bits and pieces to catch glimpses of the big picture, they will come to an understanding that the truth curiously resembles the primitive myths and superstitions held so dear by their Stage Two parents. It is at the point of catching these glimpses that Stage Three individuals begin to convert to Stage Four, which has been called the Mystical/Communal.

Stage Four individuals are referred to as mystical because they see a kind of cohesion behind physical reality. As Scott Peck puts it, "Seeing that kind of inter-connectedness beneath the surface, mystics of all cultures and religions have always spoken in terms of unity and community." In reality, what he or she has experienced is that the universe is a single organism, and that each one of us—along with every animal, tree, rock or celestial sphere—is a facet of it. Each seemingly separate part is a component of the whole, just as a nose, or a foot, is a facet of one's physical body.

Peck observed that we tend to be threatened by those in the stages of spiritual development ahead of us and by what they believe. For example, while people in Stage One may seem as though nothing bothers them, underneath they are terrified of virtually everyone, which explains why my Stage One acquaintance left so many bloody bodies in his path. Far from being frightened of them, Stage Two folks see Stage One folks as fertile ground for conversion, recognizing them to be sinners who need to be shown the light. Conversely, Stage Two people tend to be threatened by Stage Three skeptics. They are even more put off by Stage Four mystical types who seem to believe the same things they do, but with a kind of freedom they find terrifying. They usually hate to be reminded, for example, that it was their savior, Jesus Christ, who turned water into wine at the wedding when the host had run out of joy juice. They prefer to think of Jesus as serious and pious, even though the most casual reading of the Gospels reveals he enjoyed a good time as much as, or perhaps even more than, anyone else. His first miracle was to turn water into wine so the wedding celebration wouldn't end before it was time, and the hosting family would not be embarrassed when the carafes ran dry. Jesus in fact compared his ministry to a wedding feast in that it was a time for joy and celebration. There can be little doubt he considered love more important than duty or discipline.

Let's look at how the various stages view one another. Stage Threes certainly aren't threatened by Stage Ones, except when they find themselves facing one wielding a gun or a knife. They see Stage Twos as mostly idiotic zealots—harmless except for their efforts to legislate morals or to ban certain books or the teaching of evolution in the public schools. But Stage Threes are threatened by Stage Fours, who seem to be scientifically minded but also inexplicably believe in this crazy God thing. As Scott Peck says, "If you mentioned the word 'conversion' to a Stage Three individual, he or she would see a vision of a missionary arm-twisting a heathen and would go through the roof."

Regardless of the skepticism of Stage Three individuals, mystics and spiritual thinkers throughout the centuries and in all societies have believed in the connectedness sensed by Stage Four individuals. In her best-selling book, *A History of God,* Karen Armstrong writes, "One of the reasons why religion seems irrelevant today is that many of us no longer have the sense that we are surrounded by the unseen. Our scientific culture educates us to focus our attention on the physical and material world in front of us. This method of looking at the world has achieved great results. One of its consequences, however, is that we have, as it were, edited out the sense of the 'spiritual' or the 'holy' which pervades the lives of people in more traditional societies at every level and which was once an essential component of our human experience of the world."

Indeed, in the television series *Power of Myth,* Joseph Campbell said that the theme of all mythology throughout history and in every culture is the existence of an invisible plane that supports and informs the visible.

Scott Peck didn't go beyond Stage Four in his theory of the levels of spiritual growth, but I believe that at least one more stage exists. Stage Five, as I call it, might be called the Spiritual/Transient. These are folks who are so attuned to the spiritual side of reality that they are able to slip back and forth between the physical and nonphysical. Apparently, Emanuel Swedenborg (1689-1772) had this ability. Thomas Campbell, the author of *My Big TOE* (Theory of Everything) claims to have it. Mystics, from Buddha to Jesus, to the current Dalai Lama, would definitely qualify. Edgar Cayce was able to tap into the universal subconscious mind at will, simply by lying back and closing his eyes. He did this every day for forty years or more in, correctly diagnosing and offering effective cures to thousands of afflicted persons who wrote to him for help.

I've witnessed this sort of thing myself when I have visited the School of Metaphysics in Windyville, Missouri. At the gentle urging of a "conductor," trained "readers" slip easily into a trance and access the Akashic records, which are thought to be the memory of all thoughts and actions from the beginning of time—a sort of Google Cloud or hard drive data base in the universal subconscious mind.

Chapter Five
Making a Conscious Decision to Grow

Let's return to the Law of Karma. Anyone who wants to advance as quickly as possible toward the top level of heaven needs to know about it. Inherent in the Law is that the more you give, the more you will receive—that what you send out into the world will return to you. Therefore, the more you assist others, the more you assist yourself. This is not some theoretical, do-gooder idea. It will work in your day-to-day life provided your intension or motive is to express unconditional love without seeking or expecting anything in return.

You see, what you intend—your motivation—is more important than what you actually do. Edgar Cayce, for example, conducted life readings for two individuals who in the most reason past life of each had done exactly the same things but for different reasons. Edgar Cayce could tune into the Akashic Records while in trance—what in Christianity and Judaism is known as "The Book of Life" (Psalm 69:28)—and used the information to explain why. One had been motivated by personal gain, the other to bring companionship and comfort to those who lacked those things and were searching for it. One was experiencing a positive life this time around—she was revered by many as a living saint. The other's life was not going well at all. People did not trust her or respect her even though in this life she was doing nothing wrong.

When in comes to creating Karma, the intentions and motivations behind a person's actions are more important than the actual actions themselves. One cannot buy good Karma or a better place in heaven with good works or money, although in the past some people have certainly thought so. In the sixteenth century, a person supposedly could lesson the time spend in purgatory for the sins he or she had committed by making a monetary donation to the Church. The fact that the Church was selling what was then called "indulgences" led Martin Luther to break away, and the protestant reformation followed.

We are called by Jesus to love one another, and giving money or being nice so you will get something in return is not love. Consider, for example, Emanual Swedenborg, the eighteenth century theologian's definition: "Love consists in desiring to give what is our own to another and feeling his delight as our own."

Obviously, the universe knows what's up, or to modify Abraham Lincoln's famous quip, "You can fool some of the people all of the time, and all of the people some of the time—but you can never fool the Universal Mind—ever."

You get back what you deserve based on your motives and intensions.

All well and good, you say, but what if giving and expressing unconditional love is not part of your nature? Here's my advice: As I wrote before, "Fake it until you feel it." As you express unconditional love and see how it affects those who receive it, you will eventually come to enjoy giving it. As time goes by, your motive for giving it will change. You will do so because it makes you feel good.

I can sense someone reading this turning up his or her nose at the notion of loving some bum on the street, or a former enemy, or a member of the other political party. If that's you, maybe your definition of love is what's causing discomfort. Unconditional love is not romantic love. When Jesus said, "Love your neighbor as yourself," he wasn't talking about romantic love, he was talking about empathy, and about changing your actions toward them. He was talking about the Golden Rule—treating them as you would have them treat you.

The love Jesus was advocating is as much a verb as it is a noun. It means accepting people as they are without judgment or expectations—the full acceptance of others without attempting to change them, except perhaps by positive example. The law of unconditional love says, "If you go out of your way to express unconditional love, you automatically rise above fear, and, as you transcend your fears, you automatically open to the expression of unconditional love."

Still not convinced? Someone at your office is despicable and mean to you? Being kind to them is going to be extremely difficult if not impossible, is that it? Let me say that I understand it won't be easy. I've been there, and having been there, I can assure you the first thing you must do is to forgive that person. Forgive him or her, forgive yourself, and forgive others. This doesn't mean rolling over and playing dead. If you are in an abusive relationship, get out of it. Get out of it and forgive the abuser. As long as you hold onto bitterness toward someone, bitterness will come back to you. Forgive. Pray for the one who has abused you. Pray that God's peace, serenity, and love will come to that person.

Let me tell you a true story that might help. Once I worked with a man who was the most unlovable person I have ever met. It was almost impossible for me to like him. He was mean, spiteful, and petty. I'd known him a while before I found myself working with him. By a series of what seemed coincidences, he became my partner in an advertising agency. He owned the largest share, more than fifty percent, and ultimately was able to call the shots. We disagreed at almost every turn.

About six months after we came together in business, I traveled to New York to visit with the editors of *Advertising Age, ADWEEK,* and the ad columnist for the *New York Times* among others, in an effort to drum up publicity for our business. I had breakfast meetings, lunch meetings, after-work drink meetings, and was dragged from one place to another by our publicist. All of this meeting and greeting gave me a splitting headache. I'm basically an introvert and had to be "on" the whole time—not my idea of fun. But I was doing what needed to be done to benefit myself, my partner and our employees.

The morning I returned to my office in Virginia, I opened the *New York Times* to the business section and realized that lightning had struck. My picture was at the head of the advertising column. It must have been a very slow day for news in the ad game. Three-quarters of the text was devoted to our little upstart agency in Richmond. What a coup to be featured in the Gray Lady herself, where the presidents and ad managers of companies all over the United States would see us. Practically any ad agency owner would have given his first born for that kind of publicity. Reprints would be run off by the thousands and sent to every client prospect from Nova Scotia to Key West. I was ecstatic and certain my partner would be pleased.

But no, he was angry. His name wasn't mentioned in the article. How dare my name and photo appear in an article in the *New York Times* and his name not be mentioned? He was the creative director, wasn't he? His name was on the door same as mine, wasn't it? He owned more stock, didn't he?

Wait a minute. I didn't write the story, I told him. Of course I'd talked about him in the interview. I'd sung his praises. The columnist and I had talked an hour. He had selected what he wanted to write about. A lot of what I'd said had found its way onto the cutting room floor.

That didn't matter. He was not included, and it was somehow my fault. Not only was he now even more impossible to live with than usual for the next week or two, I learned later that he actually had pulled our publicist into his office, shut the door, and rather than give her the pat on the back she deserved, had threatened to fire her if another story on the agency ever appeared without his name in it.

Needless to say, having this guy as a partner was no fun. It got so bad I began to dread coming to work. Perhaps he and I had Karma from a former life to work out, I don't know. I wasn't aware of such things then. But in retrospect, I believe we would still have some to work out if I hadn't followed the course I recommend to you.

I had recently learned that one of the things Jesus told people to do was to pray for their enemies. I knew this wouldn't be easy, but I thought at least I ought to try. So, I prayed for this guy. I meditated about him and his situation. I could see the disharmony and chaos inside. He was like a nerve ending dangling and exposed, ready to touch something, anything, and streak off like a heat-seeking missile. I asked God to bring him comfort and peace. I prayed that his splintered soul would be healed and made whole. I asked God to come into his life, to slip into his heart, and to show him the way to peace and tranquility. Every time he upset me, I would pray this prayer at the first opportunity.

Something happened I hadn't expected. I found that these prayers helped me. I found that I no longer could feel animosity toward him. I couldn't harbor anger once I'd prayed for him. The anger melted. The burden lifted. I felt light, buoyant.

This would have been reason enough to have done all that praying, but to my astonishment, it was not the only good that came about. Within two months, he called me into his office and announced he was retiring. To say I was surprised would be a gross understatement. He was only 54 and had never so much as hinted at the possibility.

Doctor's orders, he said. He'd had a heart attack a few years before, and a recent stress test had revealed new blockages had reformed. They were still at the point where they could be taken care of without high-risk surgery, but his doctor had advised him to get out of the business before it killed him. He had to slow down, take it easy, and get away from the stress.

I bought his share of the business. I paid more than I should, but that didn't matter. Suddenly, my working life was a pleasure again. My brother joined me in the business and we were able to build up the agency and sell it. Enough was generated to allow me to try my hand at writing full time, which was something I'd always wanted to do. But the real kicker, the most amazing thing is, my former partner was able to do something he'd always wanted to, which was paint. Fine art was a passion he'd neglected in favor of the advertising business and the almighty dollar, and so he was able at last to devote time to his real purpose and, "follow his bliss." A feature article appeared in the paper about him a few years after he retired. He had achieved success in this new career. I imagine the blockages were a thing of the past. He certainly looked healthy. No doubt his stress level was down to almost zero, which means he had been led to the peace, tranquility, and dare I say the harmony I'd prayed that he would find.

The lesson this man taught me is to forgive. You can do this, too, by praying for whomever you feel has wronged you. Pray that they will find whatever they need to make them whole. And when you do, what seems like a miracle may happen. Rather, if you hold onto ill feelings, the animosity you harbor toward them will return to you as surely as a lead ball dropped from a tower will hit the ground.

Much good can come as a result of the law that what you give out will return to you, but keep in mind it also has a downside. If you spew hate, if you think negatively of someone, or send negative thoughts to them, the thoughts may harm the person, but in due course, they will return to you as surely as they were sent. The same is true of disharmonious deeds. Fortunately, the law works both ways, and positive thoughts, words, and deeds will return to the sender as well.

Let this be a word to the wise.

Chapter Six
Be Truthful to Yourself and Others

Our beliefs can be erroneous; yet holding onto them even though they are can nonetheless be comforting. They give us the feeling we have things figured out—and not having things figured out can be unsettling. Unfortunately, believing something is true when it is not can lead to harm, and yet even when presented with overwhelming facts, those of us with strong beliefs often are not swayed, even so. This has been demonstrated through research conducted by a man named Drew Westen, a professor in the Departments of Psychology and Psychiatry at Emory University in Atlanta.

Dr. Westen studied how people think, particularly in the area of politics. Using MRI scans, he has demonstrated that persons with partisan preferences believe what they want to believe regardless of the facts. Not only that, they unconsciously congratulate themselves—the reward centers of their brains light up—when they reject new information that does not square with their predetermined views.

In one test conducted a dozen years ago during the 2004 presidential election, subjects were presented with contradictory statements made by George Bush and John Kerry. Republicans judged Kerry's flip-flop harshly, while letting Bush off the hook for his. Democrats did the reverse. Interestingly, brain scans showed that the parts of the brain accounting for emotion were far more active during the experiment than the reasoning parts. This is why your Mama told you not to bring up politics or religion at a cocktail party attended by people whose beliefs and leanings you don't know.

Whether you realize it or not, you have a belief system. We all do. You might compare one to stack of cans like you might see in a grocery store, containing peas or soup that forms a pyramid. Each can represents an individual belief. All are in place and fit together to form a worldview, a sort of system that makes sense because everything belongs where it is and holds the other cans in place. But what happens if hard evidence turns up that refutes one of your beliefs, especially one of the key supports near the bottom? Suppose if you remove that can, the whole stack will come tumbling down?

If you're honest with yourself, that can of peas will have to go, even though you may be left with a mess. If you are a seeker of truth and harmony—if you want to graduate from earth school—you will have to remove an erroneous belief even though your pyramid may have to be reconstructed from the ground up. It's a fact that the truth can set you free, and it's a fact that denying the truth and failing to recognize and accept it—as well as leading others astray in the process— will inevitably create disharmony and problematic circumstances. On top of this, if you refuse to deal with a highly emotional issue, or refuse to take responsibility for an unpleasant situation, you are setting up circumstances that will eventually lead to an unpleasant outcome. Such an outcome can be put off for lifetimes, but the effect will be experienced in the meantime—mentally, physically, or as a lifestyle manifestation until you correctly balance the situation and restore harmony.

There are triggers to look out for that will help you recognize the truth when it comes knocking at your door. In Matthew 7:3, Jesus says, "Why do you look at the speck of sawdust in your brother's eye and pay no attention to the plank in your own eye?" (NIV Translation) Jesus knew the traits you respond to in others, are those you also have, both positive and negative. This has four primary manifestations:

1. That which you admire in others, exists in you;
2. That which you resist and react to strongly in others is sure to be found within you as well;
3. That which you resist and react to in others is something you are afraid exists within you; and,
4. That which you dislike in yourself, you will dislike in others.

One of the reasons you are enrolled in Earth School is to rise above the effects of fear. Those fears are reflected in your reactions to others. What you need to do should be obvious. Open up to the truth, recognize it, let go of fear, and express unconditional love to others who are part of your life.

A related phenomenon is known as The Law of Dissonance. It says you will experience mental discomfort and create disharmony within yourself when you hold two conflicting beliefs, or when your actions don't agree with your beliefs. For example, you may believe smoking is bad for your health, and yet you smoke. When beliefs and actions are incompatible, you will attempt to reduce your discomfort by changing either your actions, or your beliefs. As a result, you will either become a non-smoker, or you will deny or rationalize the health threat.

If you believe something to be, it becomes truth for you. Therefore, be careful what you accept as true for it will influence all aspects of your life and your future.

Chapter Seven
Always Have and Pursue a Challenge

Believe it or not, even though the physical universe derives from a single, unified force, the Universal Mind, the reality it has produced—the one we inhabit, physical reality—is constructed of opposites: yin and yang, good and evil, up and down, front and back, and so forth. As mentioned before, without the tension this creates, everything would fall apart. As a natural consequence, that which is totally successful tends to destroy itself. Most of us know this unconsciously, which is why we do not allow our relationships or careers to become totally successful. We realize that if we achieve that pinnacle, we greatly increase the potential for self-destruction.

For example, consider a couple that struggles through a number of adversities, such as getting the husband through medical school, sickness, a badly timed pregnancy, financial problems, and family troubles. Eventually, the couple arrives at a point when everything is going well. What happens? They get divorced.

A spiritual seeker who is making profound progress will often reach a point when he or she backslides and behaves negatively. The fall of cult and religious leaders and TV evangelists are cases in point. A successful business executive who has made it to the top of his or her profession often will have a mid-life identity crisis or nervous breakdown and destroy it all. Someone who inherits wealth or wins the lottery may destroy him or herself through dissipation.

In each of these examples, when total success was obtained, there was no more challenge, and destruction followed. The falls were brought about by a lack of harmony, caused by relaxed tension, coupled with the unconscious desire to experience the challenge again.

The bottom line reality is that unless a person continues to be challenged, he or she will stagnate. How many times have we seen someone who was healthy and active all his or her life retire and then quickly go downhill—perhaps even die? I saw this happen just last week. Yin and yang need to stay in balance. As previously noted, there is nothing truly solid in the universe. It is rapidly vibrating energy. When Einstein discovered that "matter is energy" he opened the door to merging science and metaphysics.

Scientists have proven that energy cannot die, it can only transform (reincarnate). You are energy. Your skin, which appears solid, is actually trillions of swiftly moving molecules orbiting each other at a specific rate of vibration. This vibrating mass must by its very nature keep moving—either forward or backward. In light of this, do not hold back. Attain total success but do not allow complacency to set in. You can do this by always seeking new challenges and by understanding that without one, self-destruction will result. By keeping success and challenge in balance, it will be possible to maintain your position and retain success. In other words, always have a challenge you are striving to accomplish, but make it one that minimizes the downside risk while simultaneously fulfilling the need for yin-yang balance. This often can be accomplished through wisely calculated risk-taking.

It can also be comforting to know there can be no growth without at least some discontent. Deep within you, at the level of your higher self, you know what is best for you. There is an urge built in to you pushes you to strive for more awareness. Suffice it to say, you ought never allow yourself to reach a level of self-satisfaction where there is an absence of challenge. For most of us, growth will not continue without some agitation and discontent. So study your dissatisfactions, for they will tell you what you are about to leave behind and possibly point you in a new direction.

Inevitably, there will be turning points in each person's life—a break in the energy wave patterns and a complete change. Everything will be affected by this change in flux, some things to a lesser degree than others. Examples include: 1) a tragedy such as the death of a loved one; 2) a religious conversion; 3) a point in therapy when something clicks and from that time on you begin to get well; 4) a mother giving birth to a baby.

For me, it was when I realized I'd gone stale in my career. I began having a recurring vision of myself coming around the track again and again. You might call it daily *déjà vu*. I'd excelled in my career—was president of my own advertising agency. I was pulling down a salary well into six figures, was listed in *Who's Who in the Media and Communications*. I had accomplished what our society and our educational system seems to indicate ought to be the primary goal of life and the one true way to happiness and fulfillment. I'd picked a profession and risen to the top. And as many who reach such rarefied air also have found, it wasn't all it had been cracked up to be.

Don't get me wrong. I love the creative process, and being creative is what advertising is all about. After a few years, I began doing some marketing communications work again. But when you are successful, and this is true in many other lines of work, after a certain point you no longer do what made you successful. You end up supervising others who get to have all the fun, while you get the headaches. That's why I've arranged my advertising and marketing activities today so that I get to do the fun part, which is working with clients and actually doing the work. That, and the ongoing need to pay my bills, creates more than sufficient tension to keep things in balance.

That's today. Back then, there was something else I'd always wanted to do, and it started calling to me. I since have found that when you want something, and remain attentive, an opportunity will appear.

In Chapter One, I introduced the concept of the Hero's Journey, and I have mentioned it a few times since. Either the hero is thrust unwillingly into an adventure, or it starts with a call. Joseph Campbell (1904-1983) labeled the latter, "The call to adventure." This call will come whether your desire is at a conscious level, or whether it's hidden in your subconscious mind. You'll be presented with a choice. You can follow your adventure and gain from it. Or you can refuse the call, in which case you will stagnate and eventually die—figuratively, or perhaps even literally. Ignoring the call is the cause of much ill health that's hidden beneath our noses. Your higher self often will use the two by four of a health crisis to get your attention, which prompts a word to the wise: To accept the call to adventure is to choose life over old age and death. In the next chapter we will take a look a real-life example of how this once played out, and we will consider how invisible forces may be at work in your life setting you up for something similar.

Chapter Eight
Follow Your Bliss

You probably know more about the hero's journey than you realize. That's because it is the underlying plot skeleton of most successful novels and films. A sympathetic lead character finds him or herself in trouble of one kind or other, and like Dorothy when she landed in Oz, she must step out of her ordinary world—literally or figuratively—into a new, often unfamiliar and frightening situation or world where she must try her best to solve the problem and before she can return home. Each effort, however, gets our hero deeper into trouble, and each new obstacle in her path appears larger than the last. Finally, when things look blackest, and it seems certain that our hero is finished, she manages to get out of trouble through her own efforts, intelligence, or ingenuity. No cavalry to the rescue is allowed. That would ruin the story for those reading or watching.

Obviously there are as many ways to put flesh on this skeleton as there are novels on the shelves at Barnes & Noble. But whether the problem the hero must face and overcome is physical, emotional, financial, or otherwise, the structure is pretty much the same. As stated previously, I believe the reason we typically find such stories compelling is that it's the story of each of us. Our ordinary world is non-physical reality. Physical reality—this earth—is not our home. We come here to fight battles, to conquer new challenges, and to rise to a higher level of understanding just as Dorothy did.

Returning to my personal story, there I was, tired of the ad game and ready to move to a higher plane, but held in place by golden handcuffs. I was ripe for the call, and naturally it came. It was not easy to turn away from that earthly treasure, but I did. I started writing. And I loved it.

Like any hero's adventure, it was frightening to take that first step, to answer the call, and the adventure became even more frightening as it continued. Soon more money was going out than coming in. I had to dip into savings in a big way. I won't bore you with a detailed account of sleepless nights and years of pinching pennies. Let it be sufficient to say I had to fight my own dragons and demons and to confront the fears that told me I ought to get my nose pressed back against the grindstone of the workaday world. But, as in any hero's adventure, when the going got really tough, unseen hands—the support of the divine—stepped in.

As a result of what I have learned from personal experience and from 40 years studying metaphysics and searching for the truth about life, my advice is to follow your bliss. This is the advice the mythologist, writer and lecturer Joseph Campbell repeatedly gave his students at Sarah Lawrence College. Whether you are just starting out, or at a turning point, it seems to me it's what you ought to do in an effort to reach your full potential in this lifetime.

How The Big Dreamer Works in Your Life

My concept of The Big Dreamer comes from the German philosopher Arthur Schopenhauer (1788-1860), who observed that specific events and the meeting of individuals, which seemed at the time to have come about by chance, later in a person's life turn out to have been essential components in a constant story line. Schopenhauer said that it is as though one dreamer were dreaming a giant dream in which each of the dream's characters has his own individual dream.

I believe, however, it's not so much that individual dreamers coordinate with each other. In truth, there's only one dreamer and one mind. Individual minds, yours and mine included, are part of it—just as radio shows are all part of a single band of frequency. Each dreamer might be thought of as an individual cell that is part of the whole. Each has a conscious mind, and each as a unique subconscious mind. But these merge into a collective mind, the Infinite Mind we all share—saint or sinner, murderer, Sunday school teacher, Ted Bundy, Buddha, or Vishnu.

We each have free will and can do things that bring pain and suffering to others and ourselves. But the Universal Mind will almost always have subsequent events work out so that at least some good will come from our ill-advised deeds. We hear the same idea expressed in a different way when people speak about God having an overall plan that we cannot possibly understand, and that, "He works in mysterious ways."

Many I have interviewed believe that on the other side, in spirit, we chose the time and place of our births, and in so doing, we determine the direction and the experiences of each life that are likely. We make many decisions about the lifetime we will be entering into. We chose our parents, we choose other souls to interact with, and some say we select the astrological configurations of our birth, which determine character, personality, abilities, restrictions, and the timing for strengths and weaknesses. If all of this seems too complicated and far out to be possible, it helps to realize our minds are part of and extensions of the Infinite Mind, which means estimates by today's experts that we use only about ten percent of our mind power are probably extremely conservative.

And something else: Each one of us has a guiding principle within that metaphysicians call Dharma, a Sanskrit word meaning "statute" or "law." Dharma is the law that orders the universe and the essential nature or function of a person or a thing. It is what we have to give or to share with others, which means that even though we may be good at something, we are not fulfilling our Dharma if we are primarily after acclaim or money. We need to use our Dharma in service to others.

I once had Dharma explained to me this way by an accomplished metaphysician whom I respect. She said, "Dharma is your soul's urge. When you are responding to your Dharma, you feel at peace. Someday, after you grow old and look back at life, you will regard the time you spent putting your Dharma to work as the golden years. This is because people who are using their Dharma are passionate about what they do, as though it were a flame burning in them. They lose track of time. They're in the flow. And something else. Each person applies his or her Dharma in a way that is unique. It is as though each of us is one piece of a giant jigsaw puzzle, and we fit together to make up a whole."

Dharma has directed your past and present life experiences, always urging you to forge ahead into activities and situations that will help form the character and the knowledge needed to fulfill your destiny. Of course, you have free will and do not have to fulfill your Dharma. But if you listen to inner direction, it will direct you to do so. The Dharmic direction each person receives is right for that person and is likely to fall into one of seven directions:

- One is work force. This path includes the majority of general occupations, including homemakers.
- Two is military. This includes soldiers and police.
- Three is service, which includes religious workers, medical, social services, counselors, and practicing metaphysicians.
- Four is creativity and includes artists, writers, poets, actors and entertainers.
- Five is science, which includes medical researchers, engineers, and technologists.
- Six is philosophy, including all who present theories about why humans do what they do.

- Seven is government and includes government leaders from president down through all areas of elected office.

Perhaps you are at a turning point and have decided to pursue your bliss, which will result in putting your Dharma to work. If so, it is time to let go of anything that is no longer useful or purposeful without regrets or resentment. This includes books, philosophy, clothing, beliefs, your lifestyle, even club memberships. Pleasure should be in the moment of the experience, and when something is no longer useful, by letting it go you free yourself to begin a new learning experience without being bound by the old.

As you contemplate your future course, it is also important to realize you can only attract that which you feel worthy of. Self-esteem is critical to success. The truth is you are not what you have, and you are not what you do. Beneath your fear programming, you are perfect—an enlightened soul, fully self-actualized and a living example of unconditional love. It is only lifetimes of fear programming that prevent you from acknowledging who you really are. The more you can let go of the fears, the higher your self esteem will be, and the more options you will have and more risks you can take. The more you like yourself, the more others will like you, and the more worthy you will feel.

You can have practically anything you want if you can give up the belief you cannot have it—assuming what you want does not conflict with someone else's belief. If, for example, you desire a fulfilling, one-to-one relationship, but demand it to be with a particular person, you are not operating in harmony with the universe.

Another example is in the area of accomplishment. You must get the education necessary to create what you want. "Where your attention goes, your energy flows." You attract what you are and that which you concentrate upon. If you are negative, you draw in and experience negativity. If you are loving, you draw in and experience love. You can attract to you only those qualities you possess. So, if you want peace and harmony in your life, you must become peaceful and harmonious.

Something else to understand is that a stronger emotion will always dominate a weaker one. Every idea you perceive is the beginning of a manifestation—although all ideas are not expressed in reality. It does not matter which idea you consciously favor, even know to be desirable, the stronger emotion will nullify the weaker ones, and the strongest emotion will begin to permeate all aspects of your activities. For example, if you are emotionally focused on the sexual desirability of a particular person, you may begin to create circumstances that will increase the likelihood of an eventual sexual union.

It is also important to realize that new information entering your mind destroys previous information of a similar nature. Once a pathway of information has been established in you, that viewpoint will prevail unless new information comes in to replace and destroy it. Let's say you fall off and get hurt while horseback riding. That may be the end of your experience with horses because you will have been programmed negatively about horseback riding. This is why instructors always urge new riders to climb back aboard the horse immediately. You need new input to erase the trauma of the fall.

The mind is engaged in an endless state of growth and reorganization. As a result, it is possible to reprogram yourself. This can be done, for example, by repeatedly listening to success-meditation recordings, or with visualization techniques. If you feel anxiety in crowds, imagine yourself relaxed in a crowd of people. When you fear doing something, and yet have the courage to do it anyway, you will soon do a mental flip-flop and may even become addicted to doing it.

Here is a case in point. Suppose you fear skydiving, or skiing straight down a steep mountain. If you force yourself to do so anyway, the experience will release endorphins, which are produced by the central nervous system and the pituitary gland and can produce a feeling of euphoria very similar to that produced by opiates. The result can be that you become somewhat addicted to skiing straight down mountains and skydiving.

Finally, when considering your new challenge, you may want to consider whether it is something you will do alone, or if it can be more readily accomplished in cooperation with others. When two or more people of similar vibration are gathered for a shared purpose, their combined energy directed toward the attainment of that purpose is doubled, tripled, quadrupled or more. Covens, esoteric religions, healing groups, and even worldwide meditations for world peace have used this phenomenon. The prolific author of personal-success literature, Napoleon Hill (1883-1970) called attention to it in his perennial bestseller, *Think, and Grow Rich*.

You have within yourself everything required to make this earthly incarnation a huge success if you choose to accept that which is your divine birthright. We live in a universe of abundance, although the majority of humans populating our planet appear to view it as a universe of scarcity. The trick is to change what you believe. That's when the reality you experience will change.

Chapter Nine
A Few More Thoughts & Truths

What else can you do to create a happier life for yourself as you work toward becoming an individual who belongs on the top level of heaven? Here are a few suggestions:

Take five minutes, twice a day to affirm your goals, dreams, and desires. Most of us do not achieve our goals, not because we are too lazy or untalented, but because we forget about them and focus our efforts elsewhere.

Spend some time in nature. Even if it is for just ten minutes a day, take the time to go for a short walk or sit in a place surrounded by nature. Release the stress of the day by communing with God's creation, and you will soon feel recharged.

Exercise. Your body is your temple. Take care of your temple every day. If your body is not in top form, neither will you be. Exercising, eating healthy and taking care of your amazing vehicle in this reality is a requirement for you to be able to produce at the highest levels.

Meditate. The biggest improvements in our lives come from within. An effective way to release the limiting beliefs and destructive thoughts that may plague you is to meditate for thirty minutes a day. Among the many benefits, meditation teaches you focus, and the success of opening to the transcendental part of yourself is strongly affected by your ability to focus. Regular practice of meditation has been scientifically proven to change your brain chemistry, lower blood pressure, make you sleep better, feel less stressed and more.

Smile a lot. A smile can change the world. Not only for you but also for the people you interact with. Practice a genuine smile and give joy to the world. Impact the world today by smiling at everyone around you.

Find more ways to have fun. Life does not have to be a strict, gloomy experience we struggle through. Instead it can be full of amazing twists and turns. Think of it as an adventure because that's what it really is. Approach it as such.

Make sure you laugh out loud at least once a day. Do something stupid, childish, and completely weird. Be yourself, have fun, laugh at your own jokes.

Remember that we are all part of one mind, a great energy gestalt, and we are connected at the level of the collective unconsciousness. On a higher self or psychic level, it is possible for anyone to tune in to anyone else and to draw upon the entire gestalt. Humankind takes advancing steps when group consciousness reaches critical mass and new awareness is accepted by the whole.

Realize that everything begins as a thought or idea. Ideas and experiences create beliefs that in turn create your reality. If you are unhappy with your current reality, you must change your beliefs and your behavior. Beliefs should be changed when you recognize which ones are not working for you.

Change that belief, and your life will change.

With respect to changing your behavior, you must first decide the disharmonious behavior you need to eliminate. Then realize you don't have to change how you feel about it, you simply have to change what you are doing. The Buddha knew what he was talking about when he said, "It is your resistance to what is that causes your suffering." By suffering, he meant everything that doesn't work in your life. This might include relationship problems, loss of loved ones, loneliness, sickness, accidents, guilt, financial hardship, unfulfilled desires, and so on. When you accept what you cannot change, you will be in position to set it aside and stop worrying about it. Like it or not, facts are facts, pure and simple. They exist, and no matter how much you resist them, there is nothing you can do about many of them. So let go. Stop holding on.

Yes, you absolutely should change what you can change—no doubt about it. But you also need to have the wisdom to accept what you cannot change. Out of acceptance will come detachment. This will enable you to enjoy the positive aspects of life without being distraction by the negative. Why waste energy focusing on things from the past when you can move on and put those things behind you?

Everyone on Earth shares the goal of soul evolution whether or not he or she realizes it. We have incarnated in order to evolve spiritually. By rising above our fear-based emotions, and by learning how to express unconditional love, we raise our vibration rate, and move closer to a state of harmony. Even when it appears we are not evolving, we are making progress. We learn through the pain our disharmonious acts generate. We learn from our mistakes and our failures. If you fell off a bicycle nine times before you learned to ride it on the tenth try, you needed nine failures in order to achieve success.

Thomas Edison conducted 10,000 experiments before he found a way to make an incandescent light bulb that worked. When asked how it felt to fail 10,000 times, he replied, "I didn't fail. I found 10,000 ways not to make a light bulb." In reality, every failure was a small success bringing him closer to accomplishing his goal. The same is true of soul evolution. Each lifetime on Earth usually has a particular purpose. It may be to learn a specific lesson. It may be to help others in some way. Some of us have missions we agreed to before we incarnated. When that is the case, the circumstances of our lives will support the pursuit and the accomplishment of that mission.

You and you alone are responsible for everything that happens to you. All is a result of your past thoughts, words, and deeds, which have formed your present attitude. Your attitude toward life and your experiences are returned to you as love and joy, or as confusion, trouble, and heartbreaking experiences. These karmic rewards and punishments can be delivered immediately, at a later date in your present life, or in a future incarnation. The way to mitigate the punishments is to grow in wisdom and to seek harmony in all that you do.

Chapter Ten
Where Will You Go from Here?

You now know that God is infinite consciousness, infinite love, infinite wisdom, and that He created physical reality in order to create you, His offspring, to become His companion and co-creator. You have been evolving toward that goal through many incarnations. Like Eve, you developed objective awareness at a point in the distant past, and from your perspective if not His, you severed your connection to the Creator. Now that you understand this, you have the opportunity to take charge of your own evolution in order to reach the goal of reunification sooner rather than later. With this in mind, let's look at another characterization of the afterlife.

Emanuel Swedenborg's View of Heaven

Jesus said his Father's house had many rooms ("mansions" in some translations, see John 14:2). Emanuel Swedenborg (1688-1772), who is reported to have been able to travel back and forth between this dimension and the next at will, maintained that non-physical reality has seven levels, with what might be considered "many rooms" in each. The top three are what Swedenborg considered heaven, the very top one being the place souls reside that have reached the apex and are in communion with God. Those who follow Jesus' Great Commandment to the letter inhabit that realm, i.e., they love God and their neighbors—not because they want something for themselves, but because they want to do so out of love for God and others.

The middle layer is situated between heaven and hell and comparable to Earth in that good and evil exist there in approximately equal measure.

The bottom three levels are ever-more intense realms of hell. Souls that find joy in doing harm to others reside there because that's where they belong and feel comfortable.

According to Swedenborg, we are not forced into any of these layers in heaven or hell, involuntarily. Rather, we create a place in one of them for ourselves because it is where we feel comfortable, and we reside there willingly. This makes sense to me. We each create our own heaven or hell on Earth and in the afterlife.

God, The Big Dreamer, Is the Force that's with You

The consciousness that is the ground of being, the organizing intelligence I have been calling God or "The Big Dreamer," might also be described as a Force that is the opposite of entropy in that it that fosters growth and evolution. I think of this Force as the hands of grace, rather than as God is normally envisioned in the West. The Universal Mind does not sit back and pick winners and losers. We individuals do so ourselves without any help from God because Karma is the law that governs our experiences. As you know by now, Karma is simply cause and effect—for every action there is an equal and opposite reaction. It's how we can learn if we will only pay attention.

Another law appears to be that life, health and harmony within an organism are supported perforce by the Universal Mind. When it comes to prayer, the more help needed, the more help that will be given. In all matters, whatever outcome will result in evolution will receive top priority. Moreover, the Universal Mind will cause events to work out in such a way that even the most horrific tragedy will produce the maximum good in the form of growth and evolution. This law was stated by the Apostle Paul in Romans 8:28, "And we know that in all things God works for the good of those who love him." That they love him means they are striving to evolve in order to become more like him. Difficulties often help us evolve, perhaps to develop empathy and understanding, and in so doing to become better people.

It cannot be over-emphasized that God does not play favorites or hold grudges. Jesus was on the mark when he said, "[God] causes his sun to rise on the evil and the good, and sends rain on the righteous and the unrighteous." (Matthew 5:45, NIV)

Additional Implications of the Truth

That subconscious mind, the builder of the body, remains connected to our Source has important implications we have not thus far discussed. For example, the experience of Edgar Cayce and other psychics indicates a patient's subjective mind is able to diagnose the character of the disease from which he is suffering and to point out suitable remedies. In addition, the subjective mind can bring about spontaneous healing, examples of which can be found in other books I have written.

Through prayer, the subjective, subconscious mind of an individual or individuals can work in concert with the Universal Mind to bring about healing, or to lessen the severity of an illness. Indeed, the beliefs held by the individual's objective mind are impressed upon his or her subjective mind with the result that the very circumstances of an individual's life will be adjusted accordingly. As has been stated, All is mind.

That the subjective mind is impersonal and is ready to assume any personality impressed upon it. Since the subjective mind is the builder of the body, it will build up a body in correspondence with the personality thus impressed upon it by a person's objective, self-aware mind. Moreover, the personality of the God our objective, ego mind believes in will be the personality of the God we have to deal with. Our subjective minds simply play back to us whatever we believe. If we assume the loving and forgiving Father God Jesus talked about, that is the God we will experience.

Our free will gives us the ability to attune our thoughts and actions with the directional force (toward growth, evolution, and harmony) of the Universal Mind. By aligning ourselves and subjugating our wills to it, we will start to "go with the flow," and life will begin to go better than if we rebel against the force of the Universal Mind. This may take effort at first, but my advice is to fake it until you feel it.

The Universal Subjective Mind brings into being what we create and hold in our objective minds. In effect, our experiences and our environment are reflections of our thoughts, feeling, beliefs and attitudes. In this way, what we hold inside becomes our reality, i.e. love begets love, hate begets hate. This is why, "What we give, we receive and what we keep we lose."

If we believe that God favors us and showers us with abundance and opportunities for fulfillment and joy, then this will be our experience. If we believe that God will punish us for our transgressions, we will indeed be punished. Our beliefs become our reality. If we wish to change our personal reality, we must first change our beliefs. The same is true in matters of health. If our fixed belief is that the body is subject to all sorts of influences beyond our control, and that some symptom or other shows that such and such an uncontrollable influence is at work on us, then that belief will impress itself on the subjective mind, and the subjective mind will proceed to fashion bodily conditions in accordance with the belief. Once we fully grasp this realization, we can see that it is as easy to externalize healthy conditions as it is the opposite.

More Implications

Your current incarnation is likely one of a long line than could possibly date back to the first life on earth or another planet. Our physical bodies are projections of the soul that has been evolving in combination with our parents genes, and those of our ancestors and our species. Some would say Earth is a kind of theme park for the Universal Mind, where it can play hide-and-seek with itself and experience the distraction of being in physical form. Because the Universal Mind is the opposite of entropy and unerringly follows laws, however, it seems more likely to me that Earth is where lessons can be learned that help us to advance in evolution.

From my studies, it also seems likely to me that souls co-operate to help one another advance. Some souls on Earth in physical form, and others in the realm of spirit, work as teachers and guides to help others advance. Still others may be ascended masters who have returned to earth from time to time to help others find the way back to God.

It makes sense to me that Jesus was the embodiment of the Christ-consciousness, which is why I have chosen to follow him. The Christ-consciousness is real and exists in spirit. Once we have attained it, we will have reached the end-goal of earthly evolution. That is why it makes sense to follow Jesus and his teachings, i.e., "to believe in him." He is indeed, "The Way, the Truth and the Life." He gave us the information we need and he set the example. He showed us the way and sacrificed himself for us in the process. No matter what path you follow, however, I believe it is important to work toward the end goal in a systematic way.

I also think that each lifetime on Earth usually has a particular purpose. It may be to learn a particular lesson. It may be to help others in some way. Some have missions they agreed to before an incarnation. When this is the case, the circumstances of one's life will support the accomplishment of that mission.

A reader of the Akashic records during a visit to the School of Metaphysics in Windyville, Missouri, once told me that I have a mission and that it is one of leadership. In striving to learn just what this mission of leadership entails, I've earnestly tried to think back as far as I can to the very first thing I can remember. Occasionally, I've had glimpses of what may be my most recent previous life. One memory is of being in an airplane, a World War II fighter. I'm the pilot. I'm in a tight bank desperately trying to outmaneuver an enemy aircraft, but my plane is hit, and I go into a spin. I don't know if this is actually a memory or a scene from some long-forgotten movie I saw as a child. Once when I was in France, however, I took a flight in a small plane piloted by a friend of my French father-in-law. The man offered to turn the controls over to me. He asked if I'd ever flown a plane.

"Never," I said.

"Here. Give it a try."

I did, and I quickly found it wasn't difficult. From the moment that I took the controls I was able to bank and turn.

The old man was amazed. "Go on," he said. "Keep going." I circled the field we'd taken off from.

"Take her down," he said. "You can do it. Land the plane."

I continued to circle until the runway was directly ahead, and then started down. A few hundred feet from touchdown, I lost my nerve, and returned the controls to him. But I'm almost certain I could have landed that plane.

My father-in-law's friend said he'd been flying more than fifty years and had never seen someone who had not flown a plane handle one as I'd just done. The vision flashed in my mind of being in the cockpit of that World War II fighter, and I could almost feel my hands on the joystick.

I've had other experiences that seem to bring back memories of former lives. There is, for example, a castle in France that gives me a strong sense of déjà vu each time I approach. It's as though I'm returning from the Crusades.

Other places in France give off a similar sense of familiarity, but they are not from the same life. They are ancient sites where Druids lived, worked, and worshiped.

I was a Druid. I can feel it as surely as I feel eyes on my back. Even though I was born in America, my life unfolded in such a way that I was led to spend a good deal of time in France so that I would remember. Writing this book is the culmination of a process that began with a life or set of lives in pre-Christian Europe. My guides are friends from that epoch. The last time I saw their faces was the moment before I left the non-physical dimension and to take on the physical body I now occupy. I can still picture my guides dressed in long, purple-gray robes. They were gathered close around me, laughing and joking. It was a kind of farewell party. They were kidding, jostling me, saying, "Don't worry, we'll be with you. Only you won't be able to see us. Not until you return." I recall being bathed in a delightful aura of love so strong that it cannot be described. And joy. Such joy. Nothing comes close.

I do not remember being born, but I do remember looking up from my crib once my parents brought me home. I did not have the sensation of being the center of the universe that logic says an infant would. I knew I was separate and unique. I recall wondering where my friends were. Their faces then flashed before me, and I felt snippets of the love and joy they had for me, and I missed them. And so began this incarnation.

As I grew, I had the feeling it was in my power to work magic. I tried my hand at magic in small ways and it worked. But as I grew, I repeatedly was told that magic did not exist. I was told that nothing existed that could not be seen. Only matter was real. In time, I came to doubt myself and to believe what I was told. As my doubts and false beliefs increased, I lost the power I once had. Only now, after many years, am I beginning to regain the power bit by bit—as I approach the completion of the mission I came to carry out.

I now have come to understand my mission is threefold: To be a guide to my sons and daughter until they no longer need me. To continue my own evolution, and to help lead others to a clearer understanding of who and what we are. That is the purpose of this book. This book represents the crux of my effort to lead others to a better and more complete understanding of who they are and what their ultimate goal ought to be.

Reflections on Lives Long Ago

In other, earlier lives, I'll bet you too knew why you were here. Long ago, when we Druids worshiped nature gods and cut mistletoe from the sacred oak tree with a golden knife, you looked up at the great arch of night sky and saw a million stars. This filled you with a sense of mystery. Do you remember, now?

In the mornings, the sun miraculously rose in the east. Its rays shot across the heavens and lit the underbellies of clouds, pink and orange. In such moments, you understood that you were one tiny facet of a wondrous creation more astounding than words could convey. You felt communion with all that surrounded you. But unlike all that, in some ways you felt separate and distinct. Even so, the owl, the deer, and other woodland creatures were your cousins, and you recognized them as such. You worshiped them, and their spirits, and they returned the favor by providing you with the food you ate and the clothes you wore and the covering for your dwelling that kept out rain and snow. The membrane that separated your mind and thoughts from the mind and thoughts of all creation was very thin—so thin that at times when you lay on your back and gazed at the stars, you felt yourself merge with your surroundings. At such times, you knew all. You knew your purpose. Creation and you were one single being. And it was ecstasy.

In time, though, you came to understand that you were different. Other creatures were driven by instincts, which were predictable. The course and timing of their migrations, their habits of reproduction and birth could be plotted like the seasons. These events were as sure to happen on schedule as the Summer and Winter Solstices. The animals had no choice. But you could behave as you pleased. You could stay another day and take a different route. You could have your babies in the fall or winter.

Even so, you lived your life in accordance with the spirit that guided you with a higher understanding than your own. To do otherwise would have been foolhardy. And if you lost touch, if you were unable to contact the Spirit on your own, the shaman or the Druid could be counted on to help you regain it.

Unconsciously, you knew your purpose. It was built into the cycles of time, of spring and summer and fall and winter, of birth and life and death and sleep. And rebirth. It was to grow and to evolve. It was to evolve and expand, to join with creation and eventually to become what you had come from. You would be a new creation. You would become so by remaining conscious of your separateness but rejoining the Source of All that Is. It was the way of nature and could be seen in the deer and the rabbit and the bear. You had become separated from the Mother of your soul as the woodland creatures had become separated from the mother of their birth. This was the Way, the wheel of life, as surely as the seed that fell to earth would someday grow into a giant oak.

But time went by, incarnations came and went, and you lost sight. You lost the sense of sacredness of All-that-Is, and you lost touch with your purpose. This was as it had to be. For your destiny was to grow and evolve to a state that encompassed all, while at the same time retaining your own personal identity. For this to be possible, it was essential that your sense of separation become strong and indelible. So you began to view the world not as one whole, but as separate pieces. It no longer seemed unified, but rather a collection of rocks, trees, individual plants and animals. Even the animals became to you as though they were constructed of distinct parts, such as hearts, eyes, kidneys and bones. You lost touch with the invisible. You ignored your intuition and the call of Spirit and came to believe the senses of the physical world provided all that you needed to know and understand. Your separation was now utter and complete. You were lost and fell into deep despair. A sense of hopelessness descended upon you.

This was necessary. You had to lose your soul before you could find and reclaim it. But the state of being lost not only is lonely, it is dangerous. Now, you and others are in jeopardy of eternal separation. If you continue on a path away from your soul, you may wander too far afield.

Life After Death

You are not alone. All humankind has reached this point on the spiritual journey. Like a flock of sheep, we are slowly climbing the mountain. Perhaps not all of us will make it. The oak produces many acorns but only a small number reach self-actualization in the form of fully-grown trees. The way is hard. It requires courage, perseverance and a willingness to change. Men and women cling to their self-centeredness. It is not easy to let go. To grow requires sacrifice. And we can become lazy, and often we are weak.

But laziness is not the only difficulty that must be overcome. We are surrounded by a culture that pushes us in the wrong direction. The one constant message is to pursue success and happiness through what seems on the surface to be the most direct route. Grab all the gusto you can get. Get your fair share. Or more. Go for the gold. These are the battle cries.

But it is fool's gold.

Not until our intuition grasps, or our experience demonstrates, the error of this thinking will the resolve come to follow the correct path. Indeed, there is hope; one branch of science, quantum physics, denies the very existence of what society tells us we should pursue—materialism. Quantum physics says there is as such as solid material stuff, but rather that matter is energy and energy is matter.

Moreover, quantum mechanics tells us all creation is one connected whole, with no separate pieces. We are the whole, and the whole is us. What happens here influences what happens there, even if it is halfway across the galaxy. Energy takes time to travel, but information is transmitted instantaneously because in truth only one mind exists.

We are creatures of the mental realm, the dimension that supports and informs physical reality. Without this realm, nothing on the physical plane would exist.

How We Can Find the Way

Your soul has evolved to its present state over many incarnations. If you do not like what you have become, you must forgive yourself and resolve to begin anew, remembering that you get back what you give. Give kindness. Receive kindness. Pay respect, and you will receive it. Bestow wealth; be wealthy. Hold love in your heart for yourself and others, and love will return to you. Hold hate or bitterness, and your life will be filled with bitterness and hate.

To change, you must forgive. You must forgive yourself as well as others.

You came into the physical world to learn this because you needed the thickness of matter to slow down the process of creating your world. In this way, you learn lessons that remain with you.

Love is what you must learn. Once you have learned to love perfectly, without selfishness or hesitation, the time for a new you will be at hand. The choice is yours. Until you learn to love unselfishly, you will continue on the wheel of life and death and rebirth.

Life After Death

Remember, too, that your fears block you as surely as do bitterness and hate. Therefore you must learn to trust. Put yourself and your fate in the hands of the Divine. Once you learn to trust rather than to fear, and once you learn to love instead of to hate, the channel between your ego self and the Infinite Mind will open wide. This will lead to a new Self.

Life is the dream of God, and you are a dreamer in that dream. You have a role or roles to play. Before you arrived in this particular life, I'm willing to bet you made a solemn vow to carry out a mission, a big part of which was to grow into the human being you have the potential to become. You can either make good on that promise, or you can welsh. If you welsh, you will view the consequences when the time comes for your life to be replayed before you, your judges, and your guides.

Or you put it down this book, forget about it, and go back to being your old self. No doubt this is what many will do. They've spent their lives doing what others said was the way to happiness and fulfillment. They may not be truly happy, but they have carved out a place for themselves. That place isn't all that exciting or fulfilling, and it can be difficult. But they've become comfortable with who and what they are. Why change?

If this is the way you feel, I doubt there's anything I can say now to change your mind. I'll tell you something from personal experience, though. There is no greater joy in life than doing what you are here to do. Getting there may be difficult, it's true. But if you listen and persevere, if you earnestly follow the path laid down, you will receive help. After a while you will begin to sense unseen hands guiding you and the way will become less difficult to find. The trials won't be as hard to bear. There will be blind alleys, of course. There will be disappointments. Sometimes, big one. There will be tough lessons to learn, but gradually you will come to a gut level understanding of what your existence as a human being is about. You will come to a gut level understanding of how you fit into the scheme. You will feel at one with it all and yet maintain your sense of self. You will come to know what you are doing. You will see outcomes materializing well before they arrive. You will choose what to pursue and what to avoid.

When you arrive at this point, you will realize that you have come to power, spiritual power, and with this realization will come joy. Can you imagine the buoyancy you'll feel? Whether it's mastery of a sport such as tennis, mastery of the card game of bridge, a musical instrument or a foreign language, the arrival at the state of really knowing what you are doing always brings joy.

It's Time to Say Goodbye

May the true riches of the universe will flow effortlessly to you because you are working with the universe, instead of rowing against the current. May your body respond to the new life you've found. No longer will there be any reason for aches and pains. No longer will there be any thought of or reason to contemplate the possibility of death, for you are on the path to Eternal Life. You will be a vibrant, living cell in the larger body of humankind, fulfilling your purpose and your promise. You will grow every day and help others do the same.

Yet with all this will come a sense of humility because you will know that it was not you that brought you to that place. It was God, and what He had in mind all along. You will be careful, therefore, and guard against feeling a sense of pride. One of the lessons you will have learned along the way is that support is withdrawn from those who believe they are accomplishing great things on their own. The saying, "Pride goes before a fall," is true. The prideful soon learn how little they can accomplish without the grace of God on their side.

Despite all this, there will be a new, deep understanding of your true worth. It will be impossible to continue to think of yourself as meaningless or insignificant once you understand that grace exists for you, that guides are constantly with you, that you and the Universal Mind are one, and that in reality you are the very Force of Life itself seeking expression and self-awareness.

In closing, let me say that my wish, my prayer, my hope is that you will put to work the special talents and gifts that only you possess for the benefit of the greater whole and for creation. My wish is that you will answer the call to adventure when it comes, and in so doing enter what Jesus called God's Kingdom.

Now you know that by answering the call you choose life over death. You now know that the forces of the universe will fold in behind you and give you their support. You will be pulled forward and pushed along by the hands of grace. All you need do is be aware, be watchful, and expect things to break your way. Stay the course. Believe. As you grow more and more attuned, as you put your talents to work in the service of others, your sense of fulfillment will begin to grow.

I feel sadness for Scientific Materialists and nihilists, whom I suppose are inevitably one and the same. If they hold on to the belief that the purpose of life is the mindless duplication of DNA, how meaningless and insignificant they must believe themselves and others to be.

They'll be in for a surprise at death. And perhaps not a happy one. Instead of the end of their consciousness, their consciousness will leave their bodies. And where will it go? A friend of mine, a psychic, won't go near graveyards because of all the confused souls who hang around the plots of ground where their bodies are planted. These lost souls don't know what to do or where to go. Contrary to their expectations, there's no end to the end of their lives.

I feel gladness, however, for you and joy that I might have been a conduit in bringing a deeper understanding of yourself. Now you know who you are, where you are going, and what the possibilities are. My sincere wish is that my efforts have helped you move another mile on the journey. Keep moving ahead. Remember always to look for the light. Expect it to be there, and it will. Go for it.

Remember always: As you believe, so will it be for you.

Stephen Hawley Martin is an author, ghostwriter, and publisher. You can learn more about him and get in touch with him through his website:

www.shmartin.com

If you found this book interesting, other books by Stephen you should know about are listed on page 2 of this book.

Intrinsic in life is an in invisible force at work creating the circumstances you deal with day after day, whether you consistently experience good fortune or ill. The author reveals the truth about this force and explains how to align and go with it to create the fulfilling and abundant life you would like to have.

Kindle: ASIN: B07JQPV4C6
Paperback: ISBN-10: 1729307906

If you think Christ Consciousness may be where we're headed, you will want to know the answers to questions this book addresses: 1) What exactly is Christ Consciousness? 2) How will achieving it make life better? 3) What can we do to begin enjoying its benefits right away? 4) What is the direct route to reach Christ Consciousness in this lifetime?"

Kindle: ASIN: B09BBD59MD
PB: ISBN-13 : 979-8544739630

Some searching for the Grail thought it was the cup Jesus used at the Last Supper. Others, a dish, or a stone. All believed it had powers to create happiness and wealth. This book explains that the True Holy Grail is secret knowledge that enabled Jesus to work miracles. This book tells that secret.

Kindle: ASIN: B07MYQ8N8V
Paperback: ISBN-10: 1794500715

You may believe humans are spiritual beings having a physical experience, but are you sure why we're here and what we ought to do about it? This book will tell this you this and much, much more because, as the record shows, the accuracy of information revealed by Edgar Cayce's more than 14,000 psychic readings was nothing less than extraordinary.

Kindle: ASIN: B08W5DL6MD
PB ISBN: 979-8706169121

Nineteen were hanged, including the author's seven-times-great grandmother, and one was crushed to death. Were their accusers lying as indicated in Arthur Miller's play, "The Crucible?" Maybe not. This book is a riveting account of a real-life murder mystery. If you'd like to know what really happened in 1692 Salem, don't miss this book.

Kindle: ASIN: B08DSTHN5Z
PB: ISBN-13 : 979-8670685528

How does the brain create consciousness? Or does it? Drawing on studies conducted at eleven universities, the author gives an answer. But be forewarned: Do not read this book if you aren't willing to consider the possible validity of research findings that may challenge some of your core beliefs about the true nature of physical reality.

Kindle: ASIN: B081LPPD8G
Paperback: ISBN-10: 1708969233

All the knowledge of the universe resides within you because at a deep level all minds, past and present, are connected. Everything that has ever happened, every thought, every idea is there. The trick is to draw out information when you need it. In this book Stephen explains how he learned to do so and how you can, too.

Kindle: ASIN: B07HHFFWP8
Paperback: ISBN-10: 1723835250

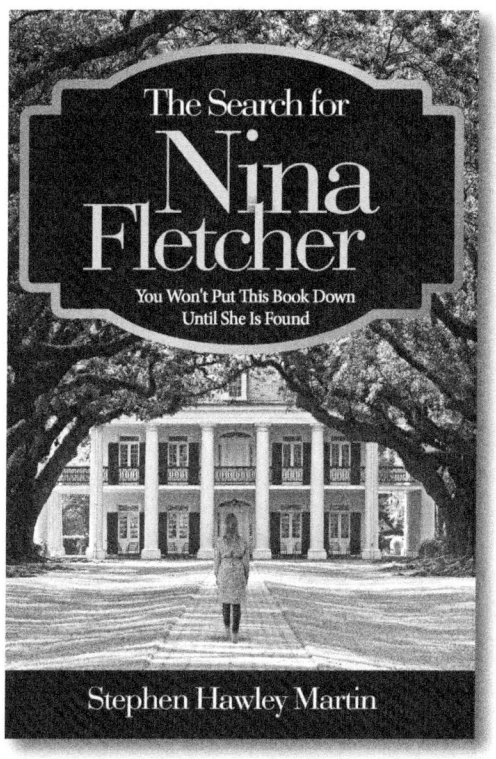

In this romantic suspense thriller, Rebecca wants to save the beautiful plantation home where she grew up, but to do so she must find her mother. If only she could remember what happened in the basement of the old house in Baltimore long ago. She must find out what happened there, she must!

Kindle: ASIN: B01J6MQZXS
Paperback: ISBN-10: 1535580879

This whodunit set in an ad agency won First Prize for Fiction from *Writer's Digest* magazine. According to Mike Chapman, Editor-in-Chief of *ADWEEK* magazine, this novel is "A thrilling and evocative read. Masterful attention to detail brings the ad agency world to life and delivers a gripping whodunit." Get ready. You won't be able to put it down.

Kindle: ASIN: B00UIGGKUA
Paperback: ISBN-10: 1511662921

Romantic suspense at its best, this fast-paced novel won First Prize for Fiction from *Writer's Digest* and First Place for Visionary Fiction from *Independent Publisher* for good reason: It's very hard to put down. You'll be riveted as Claire flies to the island of Martinique to solve a mystery and soon realizes she's being stalked by a drug lord.

Kindle: ASIN: B08S7MG4WM
PB: ISBN: 979-8591416515

Printed in Great Britain
by Amazon